ADITI
Thank you for
All that you do!

ROCKWELL

PRESS

Just Keep Sending

Ray Caughlin

D1509168

SECOND
IMPACT

SECOND IMPACT

THE RAY CIANCAGLINI STORY

ANDY SIEGEL

ROCKWELL PRESS | NEW YORK

ROCKWELL
PRESS

New York, NY
info@rockwellpress.com

Author photographs by Michael Paras
Book design by Renata Di Biase

ISBN: 978-1091193093

Dedication

This book is dedicated to all survivors of traumatic brain injury. More particularly, to those individuals who needlessly sustained a second concussion while in the recovery phase of an initial one by returning to sports competition prematurely. It is the sole intention of this work to educate young athletes, their families and those involved in organized sports about the devastating neurological consequences associated with a "second impact" brain injury. Ray, Patti and I hope to prevent even one more person from being exposed to this otherwise preventable risk of harm.

A portion of the profits from the sale of *Second Impact— The Ray Ciancaglini Story* will be donated to the nonprofit organization, The Second Impact, formed by Ray and Patti. For more information, please visit thesecondimpact.com.

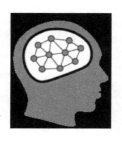

SECOND IMPACT

THE RAY CIANCAGLINI STORY
LIMITED EDITION

COLUMBIA SYNAPSE 1ST ANNUAL CONFERENCE
The Social Brain: Bridging the Brain Injury Community
COLUMBIA UNIVERSITY CAMPUS MARCH 28 - 29, 2020

On behalf of the Columbia Synapse Committee members
Ray Ciancaglini and Andy Siegel, Esq.

Please accept this book as a special thank you for your attendance.
Your participation and allyship are of great benefit to the
community of individuals with brain injury.

Conference Committee:
Shariq Jumani
Bertina Kudrin
Masih Tazhibi
Kyri LePree
Sam Dhanani
Chinmayi Balusu
Linghao Kong

Community, Neuroscience, Advocacy

Mission Statement

Ray's mission is to tell everyone about the mistake he made in ignoring the symptoms of a concussion and the lifelong consequences he has suffered as a result. Ray's goal is to raise awareness, offer support, and encourage young people to be honest with caregivers, rather than "playing through" a head injury.

Ray hopes, through his speaking engagements, that student athletes will come to understand the importance of addressing a concussion promptly and appropriately. He encourages student athletes to be honest about symptoms of concussion, and he advocates following school or sports program protocols and doctors' orders to ensure a safe return to play.

The game you sit out today could be the career you save tomorrow.

Foreword

I am a personal injury lawyer in New York City who has spent the better part of his career representing courageous survivors of traumatic brain injury. When I was retained to represent my first traumatic brain injury (TBI) client, what I met was a person not focused on seeking money for injury, but rather a profoundly compromised individual who was looking to get better.

With no one to orchestrate the course of his recovery, my lawyering took a back seat to a greater challenge, which was navigating the medical world to find him the specific help he needed. The same thing happened with my second TBI client. This pattern continued to repeat itself, and I quickly became an expert in the care, treatment and rehabilitation of brain injury. Today, my place in the legal community is not only as an advocate, but also as a medical coordinator.

Commitment and passion in litigating TBI cases has also resulted in extraordinary courtroom successes. Lawyers from all over the city refer their TBI clients to me, recognizing this complicated injury demands the involvement of a tenured legal specialist to achieve full justice. Especially so when the injured party may appear uninjured on the surface, which is why TBI is known as the invisible injury.

Before long, I found myself involved with the traumatic brain injury community on many different levels, including sitting on the board of directors of the Brain Injury Association of New York State, performing legal case presentations to the neuropsychology interns at NYU Rusk Institute, and organizing a fundraiser for the Hospital for Special Surgery Department of Rehabilitation Sports Concussion program, to list a few.

I authored the Tug Wyler Mystery Series, a collection of medical-legal thrillers, and with my debut novel, Suzy's Case, I was able to put a human face on a reality I know so well from my work life: the intensity of the experience of TBI survivors and their families. The story is so compelling that it was selected by *People* magazine as a "Best Beach Read" and optioned by CBS Television.

In 2014 I was an audience member at the Brain Injury Association of New York State's annual conference when Ray Ciancaglini gave his compelling keynote address to a packed house in Albany. Later that evening I spoke with him and Patti, and immediately appreciated that they were no ordinary couple, but rather a dynamic duo with a shared mission.

To the benefit of all, and with Patti at his side, Ray has made the most of his life situation through his crusade to educate others about concussion and the avoidable devastation of sustaining a "second impact." For definitional purposes, when Ray was a teenager, he sustained a concussion in a boxing match. Failing to appreciate the significance of his symptoms, coupled with the misconception that you had to be knocked out to sustain a concussion, he stepped into the ring again the following week. During that fight, he suffered a second concussion while still in the recovery phase of the initial one. The effects of this "second impact" altered his existence.

I wrote this book because Ray's life is a story that needs to be told for the health, welfare, and safety of all.

Second Impact is a quasi-memoir, based on Ray's recall of his experiences. Each "Round," or chapter, recounts some of these experiences, written in the third person, and ends with Ray's comments on those events. This format allows the reader to follow the story in the form of a novel and yet benefit from Ray's insightful reflections in retrospect.

The Tale of the Tape
Ray Ciancaglini

Age:	20
Weight:	160
Height:	5'8"
Reach:	67"
Chest Normal:	44"
Chest Expanded:	46"
Biceps:	16"
Forearms:	13"
Thigh:	23"
Calf:	16"
Neck:	16"
Waist:	32"
Fist:	12"
Brain:	Chronic Traumatic Encephalopathy

Belhurst Castle
Geneva, New York
November 2011

Patti's sight is trained on Ray. She's watching him intently, the way she always does just before he speaks to an audience. Across her face is the unmistakable expression of a loving wife's concern. She takes a deep breath and slowly exhales, thinking he looks good in that suit. So hearty, no one would ever suspect. But what it's covering is a battered man degenerated beyond his sixty years. Way beyond.

He's here to share the reason for his deteriorated state with students. To warn them.

Ray's breathing, uneven and choppy, reveals his anxiety. But it's a stoic uneasiness. He stands motionless over a cheese platter and several bottles of water on top of a folding table in a small makeshift green room. As he reaches for a bottle, his right hand shakes uncontrollably. Using his other, he slowly guides his quivering limb up against his chest and across his heart. He slowly closes his eyes, the way someone does in acceptance of their life circumstances. As they open, he sees Patti stepping closer to him.

"Don't worry. You'll do fine." She says in a comforting tone.

Ray manages a smile. Then, looking past her, his focus zeroes in on the wall clock. There's one in every standby room. It's in the usual location above the entry door. This one has a quartz movement.

Patti turns her head, following his line of sight, and wonders, *What's Ray thinking when he stares at a clock before going onstage?*

Ray watches the second hand, moving one loud *tick* at a time. It's the only sound in the room. *Tick, thirty-seven. Tick, thirty-eight. Tick, thirty-nine.* Ray winces.

Turning back to him, Patti softly takes his hand, guiding his arm down from his chest. "Ray, look at me."

He continues to focus on the clock. Each *tick* seemingly louder than the last. *Tick, fifty-one. Tick, fifty-two. Tick, fifty-three . . .*

"Ray. Look at me," she softly cradles his face between her hands, attempting to guide it toward her.

Resisting, he maintains his attention on the stop-and-go of the clock's second hand. *Tick, fifty-seven. Tick, fifty-eight. Tick, fifty-nine* echoes through his head as his mind submissively drifts back in time.

The hand strikes twelve.

Ding!

"Ray! Look at me!"

Memorial Auditorium
Buffalo, New York

June 1967

"Ray! Look at me!" barks Monsignor, a large man in his early six-ties, as he squats in front of Ray. Lip, who is fifty-three, squirts water into Ray's mouth from the side.

Ray—sixteen, handsome, fit, and fierce—sits on a stool in his corner, sweaty, winded, but unscathed. Wearing a con-fident grin, he continues to look past Monsignor across the boxing ring, eyeballing his opponent, Luther—seventeen, large and muscular—his face bloodied and his right eye badly swollen.

There's a moderate-size crowd in Memorial Auditorium, still cheering from the high action that ended the round. Ven-dors shout, "Popcorn! Peanuts!"

"Ray, look at me!" Monsignor repeats.

Ray spits the water into a bucket, his eyes still locked on Luther.

Monsignor grabs Ray's face between his hands and yanks so they're eye to eye. "Listen! He knows you got him. He's gonna come in head-huntin.' Finish him. But keep your guard up."

Ray gives a confident nod.

The hammer whacks the bell on the table where the time-keeper sits.

Monsignor releases Ray's face, giving it a fatherly pat as Ray pops up. Lip quickly grabs the stool.

"Get it done!" Monsignor orders as he slips through the ropes and out of the ring.

The referee keeps a steady eye as the boxers advance to center ring. Not wasting time, Ray catches Luther with a quick right followed by a powerful overhand left, staggering him back against the ropes. Luther's face leaks blood as he's attacked with a barrage of body blows. Going up top again, Ray nails Luther's puffy eye, dropping him sideways to the canvas, blood spurting now. The ref directs Ray to a neutral corner, then begins an exaggerated finger count over Luther. "Two... three... four... five..."

At *six*, Luther rises unsteadily.

The ref hand-checks Luther's gloves, giving him a quick once-over. "You good to go?"

Bloody, shaky, Luther responds, "Hell yeah."

The ref steps back and gives them the hand signal. "Fight."

Ray bullets two jabs, knocking Luther off-balance and popping his head back. Ray glances at the ref, as if to say, *Call it. This guy's toast.* No response. Ray takes a sharp step back and readies the release of his fight-ending punch. As it goes into motion, Luther throws a wild, thunderous left hook, catching Ray hard behind his right ear, throwing him off-balance but not down. The crowd jumps to their feet at the immediate change of events as Ray falters to the side with Luther closing in.

Ray, his vision blurred and doubled, his hearing impaired with the audience noise fluctuating from loud to muffled, barely brings his opponent into focus as Luther closes in for the kill—about to throw *his* knockout punch. Still confused, Ray manages a desperation uppercut, hitting flush the underside of Luther's chin, knocking him to the canvas.

The ref directs Ray away and picks up his count. "Three, four, five, six..."

Opening Comment: Ray Ciancaglini

Everybody knows boxing is a brutal sport. I mean, I knocked the crap out of that poor fella down on the canvas. Savage as it may be though, it teaches a man about character, humility and work ethic.

Any normal man in Luther's position, when asked if he's ready to continue after what I put on him earlier, would answer, *No, I've had enough of this beating.* But, to be a boxer, you need heart. And the size of a boxer's heart is measured by his desire to keep punching and his courage to fight back fear. Maintaining focus, however, regardless of heart or ability, is the difference between a contender and a champion.

The word on the street about Luther was that he was most dangerous when hurt. Something I lost focus of, out of ill-placed concern. There's no room for compassion inside a ring, so I take responsibility for that punch, having let my guard down.

But that blow—that *first impact*—instantly redirected the course of my existence in a way I could have never imagined.

But I'm way ahead of myself. My story began a decade earlier on September 23, 1957. So let's start there . . .

ROUND 1

A quaint brick-faced neighborhood eatery, Raymond's Italian Restaurant, sits midblock in a bustling part of Geneva, New York. A neon Schaefer Beer sign occupies the window to the right of the entrance, and a large poster with two boxers squaring off fills the window to the left. Two men passing by stop to read the poster.

GILLETTE FRIDAY NIGHT FIGHTS IS PROUD TO PRESENT:
CARMEN BASILIO VS. SUGAR RAY ROBINSON
FOR THE MIDDLEWEIGHT CHAMPIONSHIP
BETTER THAN RINGSIDE: SEPTEMBER 23, 1957

The restaurant is spacious inside, with ten tables, five booths and a sizable bar area. It's currently empty of patrons.

"That's final!" exclaims Ray's mom—pretty, in her mid-thirties—as she wipes down the tables with her wily, cute six-year-old, readying the place for the dinner rush.

Ray stops wiping and shoots her a look. "But, Ma!"

"You're too young!"

Ray throws his cloth on the floor defiantly. Mom gives him an angry stare. Ray quickly picks it up and continues wiping to avoid further trouble, adding, "It's not fair!"

"Irene, just let the kid watch the fight," chimes in Grandpa, who owns the restaurant bearing his name. The old man is classy and sharp, in his sixties, with a thick Italian accent. He carries a case of wine through the dining room toward the bar.

His daughter-in-law shoots him a not-so-nice look.

"What? What's the big deal?"

"I have other children to tend to at home. You just keep this child away from the TV here."

Grandpa rolls his eyes and then smiles as he puts the wine on the bar.

. . .

Later that evening Ray's father Angelo, in his early thirties, is behind the bar adjusting the rabbit ears on the black-and-white Admiral TV, which is shelved up high. The restaurant is loud, noisy and packed to watch the fight.

"Come on, Angelo!" a patron anxiously yells. "The fight's about to start! Move outta the way!"

Hand gesturing, Italian style, Angelo responds. "Hey! What's a matter wit' you?"

The patrons roar when local boy Basilio is introduced as the challenger and boo the champ, Sugar Ray Robinson. After center-ring formalities the bell sounds, starting the fight, and the boxers go toe-to-toe.

Ray, wide-eyed and mesmerized, stands off to the side, transfixed by the TV. Every time the crowd cheers, Ray's eyes get wider, and his mouth opens a little more in awe. A woman there with her father notes Ray's fascination as he stays glued to the TV, round to round, every so often air-boxing, right to the end of the fight. At the final bell, the battered boxers take their corners, exhausted.

"Hush, hush," Angelo says to the customers as the boxers take center ring for the decision. "Be quiet, everybody. Be quiet."

"This has been every bit the war we were all expecting," the ring commentator begins. "Fifteen rounds of grueling, punishing, heartfelt boxing."

The deciding scorecard is announced, and the ref raises Carmen Basilio's arm in a split-decision victory. The restaurant patrons go wild, cheering and hugging.

Standing still within the commotion is Ray. He's spellbound by the TV showing the Basilio camp celebration. "That's gonna be me one day," he whispers to himself. "That's gonna be me."

. . .

It's not long before the restaurant is empty. Grandma sweeps the floors; Angelo washes beer mugs behind the bar, and Grandpa's asleep at a table. An unfamiliar knocking comes from the kitchen. Grandma and Angelo glance at each other, sharing a questioning look. She leans the broom against the wall and enters the kitchen through a set of swinging doors.

Ray, with his back to Grandma, is punching a large linen bag propped up on a wood high-back chair. He's acting out the fifteenth round, calling the fight just as the announcer had.

Grandma puts her hands on her hips. "Ray, what are you doing?"

He ignores her, continuing to punch the laundry bag.

"Ray!"

"I want to be just like Carmen Basilio when I grow up," he responds, still punching.

"You'll be no such thing," she states firmly, raising her voice. "You're going to college, and you'll be a doctor or a lawyer."

"But, Grandma!" He pleads, now turning around.

"What's all the yelling?" Grandpa asks, entering the kitchen.

"The boy says he wants to be a boxer. Tell Ray to get that crazy idea out of his head right now."

"Why don't you finish in the restaurant? I'll talk to him. Ray, help me take these linen bags down to the basement."

Grandma turns to leave as Ray says, "But, Grandpa, I want to be a boxer."

Grandma stops and turns. "Did you see Basilio's face? Huh, Ray? Did you see his face at the end of the fight? It was a mess. And he won. Is that what you want for yourself? You want to be a champ with a mess for a face like a plate of spaghetti with tomato sauce?" She leaves.

"Take this and follow me," Grandpa says, handing Ray the linen bag off the chair and picking up two others. The basement door creaks as it always does, and down the stairs they go.

Now in the large, dimly lit area, they head toward the washer and dryer. Grandpa unloads his bags into the washer. He turns to see Ray taking the dirty tablecloths out of his bag.

"Not so fast," Grandpa says, stopping him. Ray looks up. Grandpa pulls over a large old pickle barrel and sits on its edge. "Hand me those," he says to Ray, pointing at a pair of pizza oven mitts resting on top of folded cloths on a side table. Grandpa puts them on, then holds up his hands. "Let's see what you got. I've loved boxing since I was your age."

Ray smiles.

"I'll call the punch. You throw it."

Ray nods.

"Right," calls Grandpa.

Ray throws a punch smack into the middle of the oven mitt, pushing back Grandpa's hand.

"Not bad. Again, but this time, step in as you throw it . . . Now give me a right, left, right," Grandpa says, with Ray jabbing on each signal. Impressed, Grandpa's smile grows. "Give me two rights and a left."

Smack, smack, smack!

"You're a natural, kid."

Ray's smile widens.

"Let me see an uppercut."

Ray's fist comes up, slamming into the oven mitt. *Smack!*

"Wow, you got the goods, kid."

"You think so, Grandpa?"

"I know so. You can be a contender."

Just then the creak of the basement door can be heard from up above.

"That sure don't sound like talking Ray outta boxing to me, Grandpa." Grandma's voice echoes down the basement stairs.

"*Um*, we were just finishing up." Grandpa puts his mitt to his mouth to indicate that Ray should keep quiet.

"The boy has to go home. Let's go."

"Be up in a minute." Grandpa waits for the door to shut. "Listen, Ray. You got some skills there for a puny seven-year-old."

"You think so, Grandpa? And I'm six."

"I said it once and I'll say it again, I know so."

"Hold up the mitts again. Just a little more." Grandpa looks to the stairs, then back to Ray. "One last punch. Please." He holds up his right mitt. Ray throws a right cross, and Grandpa quickly counters with a light left hook to the top of Ray's head, finishing off the playful whack by messing up his hair.

"Hey! Grandpa!"

"Boxers hit back. Laundry bags don't. Always watch out for that left hook."

The basement door creaks open again. They look over. "Grandpa! Upstairs! Now!"

Grandpa glances at Ray and they share a chuckle. He grabs Ray by his wrists, pulling him close. "Before you get good with these," Grandpa whispers, lightly making Ray punch himself in the face, "you have to get good with what's inside your head. Your grandma's right. School first. Boxing second." Grandpa pulls Ray in closer and kisses the top of his head. Now reaching into his pocket, he pulls out a few bills and hands them to Ray.

Ray stares at them for a second and then gives Grandpa a questioning look.

"You did a good job helping today. A man needs to be paid for hard work. Put that away. Save it for something special."

Ray tucks the money into his pocket and gives Grandpa a giant hug.

Grandpa squeezes him and whispers in his ear, "Our little boxing lesson is between you and me. *Capisci?*" The happy little boy nods.

"Grandpa! Ray! Upstairs! Now!"

Grandpa lifts his brows, smiling. Ray smiles back. They head up the stairs, where Grandma is waiting, holding the door open as they exit.

"Give him no ideas. He should be focused on books, not boxing." She kisses the top of Ray's head as he walks by. "Someone in this family's going to college to be a doctor or a lawyer." As Grandpa passes, she gives him a stern look. "I'll deal with you later."

Comment: Ray Ciancaglini

My journey began as innocent as can be—an enthusiastic little boy who felt the electricity generated by a title fight on television in a barroom filled with cheering fans. Everybody was smiling and laughing and having a good time—all seemingly created by a man in the ring who they were rallying behind. Yeah, he was bashed up, but it seemed worth it when the crowd erupted when they raised Carmine's hand in victory. Little did I know!

A pickle barrel and pizza oven mitts: I'd suggest these are the two most unlikely items you would associate with an irreversible, progressive, neurodegenerative brain injury leading to a life of struggle. But that's what they represent to me. And ironically, they also symbolize the best memories a little boy could ever have about his loving grandfather.

ROUND 2

On this industrial street lined with warehouses, two homes in varying stages of disrepair sit right next to each other. In one is nine-year-old Ray. He's rubbing the morning crust out of his eyes. Above him, taped to the wall, is the Basilio versus Sugar Ray poster from the restaurant window. It's surrounded by several other boxing posters. Two schoolbooks rest on a bedside table next to a stack of *The Ring* magazines. The issue on top with Basilio on its cover is Ray's favorite.

Ray looks to the single bed and crib where his two younger brothers sleep. Both are empty, a sign he'd better move quickly or risk missing breakfast. So he gets dressed and heads downstairs with an enthusiastic pop in his step.

Sitting around a small kitchen table are his two older sisters and two younger brothers, the little one in a high chair. Mom puts out some toast, and the girls butter their slices. Ray enters and snatches a piece from his sister's hand.

"Hey! That's mine! I just buttered that."

Ray looks at her, then at the toast, taking a quick bite. "That's weird. It tastes like mine."

"C'mon, Ray!"

"I'll butter yours tomorrow and the next day. I got to hop." He heads out the door.

"Where are you going?" Mom screams after him.

"Bobby's."

"Stay out of trouble."

"Always."

"And don't do anything stupid!"

"Never."

. . .

The rooftop access door flies open, startling the pigeons. Ray comes bursting through, followed by goofy Anthony, Bobby and chubby, sweet Frankie.

"Race to the end!" Rays shouts out. "Last one gets . . ."

"To eat my shit," Bobby says, sprinting and getting a head start on his pals.

Ray turns on the burners and quickly catches up, while Anthony and Frank watch, meandering behind. The two competitors are sprinting across the rooftop, side by side. As they approach its end, Ray shouts, "First one over to the next building wins!"

Bobby shoots him a concerned look, pulling to a stop just before the roof's edge, as Ray leaps to the adjacent building, lands, and turns back to his buddy, throwing his hands up in the air.

. . .

Not long afterward, Ray, Anthony, Bobby and Frankie exit Smaldone's Variety Store, munching from bags of potato chips, and head down the sidewalk. Unnoticed behind them, the nose of a police car pulls up to the intersecting corner a short distance away.

"What if you had missed?" Anthony says.

"It was a three-foot gap. Give me a break."

"You would've gotten a break all right. If you didn't make it, that is," Frank adds.

"C'mon. My grandma coulda made that jump."

Two older boys, about fourteen, walk down the sidewalk toward Ray and his friends.

"I don't know . . . I just . . . I think . . ." Bobby says.

"*I, I, I* . . . You sound like a sissy," Rays says.

"That's because he is one!" says one of the older boys, grabbing the bag of potato chips out of Bobby's hand on the pass-by without breaking stride.

"Hey!" Bobby blurts out in an excited high tone.

"Thanks for the chips, sissy boy."

"Very funny," Ray says. "We'll take those back now." The older boys stop and turn.

"You want them? Come and get them."

"I'd prefer if you just gave my friend back his chips. We're not looking for trouble."

"'You'd prefer' . . . Such nice manners. Here they are." The much bigger boy holds out the bag.

Ray steps closer, looking up at him.

Anthony, Bobby and Frank stay put.

As Ray reaches for the bag, the boy throws a punch. Ray evades it, then counters with a right to the boy's gut, doubling him over. Ray starts at the other kid, who puts up his hands in surrender. Ray turns back to the first boy, still hunched over, trying to get his breath, who juts his arm out to the side, offering up the bag.

"Take your chips back, Bobby," Ray says. As Bobby takes the bag, the police car turns the corner, pulsing its siren as it pulls up to them. The two older boys scurry off. Anthony, Bobby and Frank dart away in the other direction. But not Ray. He waits patiently. Officer Maloney—mid-thirties, short, stocky—gets out and approaches him.

. . .

Grandpa sits on the pickle barrel with a large box of peeled potatoes resting next to half a bag of unpeeled ones. Ray stands nearby, holding two pairs of pizza oven mitts. Grandpa grabs a windup timer off the counter and sets it to three minutes. He turns to Ray. "What did he say?"

"Nothin'. Just asked my name and stuff. I don't know. I was pretty scared."

"No, you weren't. You stayed. The ones who ran were scared. You were nervous. Cops can make people feel that way, especially in a situation like that."

"I guess."

"You know your mother will kill us if the cops pick you up for fighting. That's the day this ends." Grandpa gestures toward their makeshift sparring setup.

"I know."

"And, like we discussed, the need to get physical is your last option."

"Yes. I mean, we could've walked away and let that kid have Bobby's chips—"

"No, you couldn't," Grandpa states emphatically. He now looks toward the stairs and then back at Ray. "It's a matter of principle. You got him good though, right?"

"Yeah. I got him pretty good. I mean, I just wanted Bobby to get his chips back." Ray hands Grandpa one pair of mitts. They playfully stare each other down as they put them on.

Grandpa pushes himself off the barrel and takes a ready stance in the middle of the open basement. Ray squares up to him, and Grandpa gives him the nod.

Ray goes at him with vigor.

Grandpa eats what Ray has to offer. He blocks the next two punches and quickly gives him a left hook, hard across the side of Ray's face. "I'll say it again. Always be ready for that left hook."

Ray nods and comes back at Grandpa even harder. Just as he's about to throw a left hook of his own, the basement door creaks open from above.

They abruptly stop, and Grandpa, breathing heavily, puts a mitt to his lips, indicating *silence*.

"You two best be peelin' potatoes!" Grandma calls down.

"Of course we are, dear." He gives Ray a playful wink. The timer goes off—*ding*!

"Sounds to me like that's the end of peeling potatoes, Round One. Don't forget to bring my mitts upstairs when you're done. Peeling potatoes, that is." The door slams shut.

They share a warm smile. Grandpa, a bit winded, sits himself on the old pickle barrel and holds up his hands. "Let's see it."

Comment: Ray Ciancaglini

In hindsight I realize Grandpa was right. I wasn't scared. In fact, I never really knew what fear was. I had a craving for high intensity situations and met them head-on, even when the odds were against me. It was a trait that turned from ally to foe. But that's just how I was wired.

ROUND 3

From the sidewalk, three well-groomed eleven-year-old boys in Catholic school uniforms look into Smaldone's Variety Store. They watch Ray. He's kneeling, sorting through the just-delivered stack of magazines next to the string-bound newspapers.

"Come on, Ray! You're gonna make us late again," Bobby yells in.

"Yeah, hurry up. I don't want to get detention because of you," adds Frank. With no response coming from Ray, Frank turns to his companions. "Come on, fellas. He'll catch up."

"You want me to wait for you?" Anthony asks.

"Nah, go ahead. I don't want to get you in trouble."

Anthony runs to catch up to Frank and Bobby.

The magazines are now sloppily scattered on the floor under the periodical rack. Ray hears a toilet flush. "Crap," he says under his breath.

Mr. Smaldone steps out from the back bathroom, drying his hands. He looks over, gives a disapproving nod, tosses the paper towel into a wastebasket and approaches Ray. "Mama mia, Ray! You making a mess outta my store! I got it. I got it already. You put that stuff back, and I give it to you. You don't think I know by now?"

"Sorry, Mr. Smaldone. You were in the bathroom, and, well, I got to get to school, so I was looking for it myself." Ray quickly restacks the magazines.

Mr. Smaldone, having gone behind the counter, comes around, his left hand behind his back.

Ray stands and turns, addressing him. "Well?" Ray asks.

"Well?" Smaldone counters.

"Oh, yeah," Ray responds. He hastily reaches into his pocket, coming out with a handful of change. He counts out the nickels and pennies, while placing them into Mr. Smaldone's outstretched palm. "Thirty-three, thirty-four, thirty-five cents. There you go." Ray eagerly looks up.

Smaldone whips the magazine around from behind his back.

Ray grabs it and bolts out the door, leaving Smaldone smiling and amused. Ray keeps up a high-paced jog until Saint Francis Catholic School comes into sight. He sprints toward the main entrance, having just witnessed its official closing. "Oh, crap!" Ray races up the steps, through the door, and down the hall, coming to an abrupt stop at his classroom door. He shakes out his arms and shoulders, does a one-two jab and a punch, takes a deep breath, then enters Sister Saint Zita's classroom. Composed.

Sister Saint Zita, in her early thirties, turns from the blackboard toward the opening door. With a disapproving look, she watches Ray enter, lifting a brow when their gazes meet. Ray timidly walks to his seat in the back row, locking eyes with Anthony, who gives him a *you're in trouble* look. Ray sits, knowing he'll get detention for sure.

Sister Saint Zita, turning back to the chalkboard, writes, "The Seven Seas" as twenty-five well-behaved students watch. "Class," she says, turning around, "take out your geography books and open to Chapter Five on page seventy-two." The students simultaneously take out their books, put them on their desks and comply, with Ray slyly slipping a magazine inside his book upon opening it.

"Who can tell us the names of the seven seas?"

Patti—cute, blonde, confident—quickly raises her hand. Several other students raise their hands as well. Ray shoots his up, enthusiastically waving it around.

"Ray, I can see fine. No need to wave your hand about. Patti, please tell us the names of the seven seas."

Patti smiles proudly. Ray buries his face in his textbook.

"Okay, there's the Pacific Ocean, the Atlantic Ocean . . ."

As Patti continues, Sister Saint Zita silently strolls toward the back of the room.

"The Indian Ocean . . ."

Ray, head down, remains focused on his textbook-concealed magazine, while Sister Saint Zita, meanwhile, has quietly circled around the back row and now stands directly behind him, casting her shadow onto his desk.

Ray looks up, surprised.

Sister Saint Zita puts out her hand. Ray places his magazine in it, with the other students watching, including Patti, who had just named the seventh sea.

"That's correct, Patti. Great job."

Patti's face fills with pride.

Sister Saint Zita, now at the head of the class, puts the magazine in her top desk drawer, closing it shut firmly, making a statement.

. . .

Later in the day, the playground is crowded with multiple age groups. The activities spill into the parking lot, where young girls jump rope and play hopscotch. Boys play basketball as Ray, Bobby, Anthony and Frank hang out near the jungle gym. Frank's attention is caught by some goings-on at the basketball court. Following Frank's line of sight, Ray looks over.

Carlos, a thirteen-year-old physically mature transfer student, has just taken the basketball, breaking up a two-on-two game played by nine-year-olds. He's using it as a soccer ball, kicking it into the fence.

The four little boys plead with Carlos to give the ball back. He ignores them, continuing to kick it into the fence until it bounces away from Carlos, right into the hands of one of the boys. Carlos steps toward him, making a threatening gesture to the much younger and smaller kid who, scared, gives the ball back.

Ray walks over to Carlos with Anthony, but Bobby and Frank stay where they are. "Hey, Carlos. How've you been?"

"Been good." His accent is thick.

"Great. Listen, you can't break up a basketball game like that. It's not right."

"Who says?"

"Well, I do. It's common courtesy."

"But there's no soccer ball."

"I know. But Father McDonald told you that he'd get one when you took the basketball away from these kids yesterday."

"Well, I don't see no soccer ball, so I'll just use this."

Ray grabs the ball out of Carlos's hands, turns and tosses it to the boys, who are now watching Ray's intervention.

Angered, Carlos throws a sucker punch at the back of Ray's head, but Ray senses and evades it. Carlos follows with a left hook. Ray dodges that and steps toward Carlos, landing a hard body shot right to his ribs. Carlos winces. Ray and Carlos are now encircled by students, chanting, "Fight! Fight! Fight!"

The yelling catches the attention of Sister Saint Zita and Father McDonald, who are standing near the building. "Oh, no, Father. Come on. Let's go," says Sister Saint Zita.

Father McDonald, who is in his late fifties and has a muscular build, does not respond.

Upset at his inaction, she steps forward to intervene. Father McDonald gently grasps her arm. She looks down at his hand, then back up at him. He releases his hold on her. "Let them resolve this themselves."

"That's ridiculous."

"It's not."

"Why are you letting Carlos, who's twice Ray's size, beat him up?"

Father nods over to them "Because he's not."

Ray dances around Carlos, making him swing and miss. With each miss, Ray delivers one to Carlos's ribs.

"Still, you can't let them fight like delinquents."

"I can."

"Why would you?"

"I'd rather have them get their frustrations out of their system in front of me than have it carry on somewhere else."

Ray now puts up his hands in surrender. "Enough, Carlos! Enough! I don't want to hurt you."

Carlos ignores Ray's plea, continuing to throw wild punches that Ray evades.

Left with no choice, Ray throws another hard blow to the same rib area, doubling Carlos over.

Father McDonald decides it's time. He quick-steps to the fight, pushes through the crowd and between the fighting boys, breaking it up. "Recess is over for you two. March to my office now. And not one word from either of you."

■ ■ ■

After having said what needed to be said, Father McDonald pushes off his chair and stands behind his large desk. Ray and Carlos, sitting in chairs in front of the desk, look up at him. "I believe I've made myself clear. Now, you two, on your feet."

Ray and Carlos stand.

Father McDonald comes around the desk and stands between them. "Now shake hands."

Ray extends his hand. Carlos gives Ray a genuine hand-shake. The boys nod at each other again and then set their focus on Father McDonald.

"Well done, gentlemen. But there will be detention for this behavior. Carlos, you head back to class."

He nods and starts for the door.

"Straight to class."

"Yes, Father."

"Sit back down, Ray." Father McDonald sits on the edge of the desk and stares at Ray for a moment. "That's your second altercation this year. You can't solve everything with your fists."

"I know, Father. It's a last resort, but it just keeps heading in my direction. I mean, I can't stand by and watch defenseless little kids get taken advantage of."

"I understand that, son. Look. I was a marine. I see the respect you show your peers. You're not in trouble for being righteous. Now who taught you to fight like that?"

"My grandpa."

"He was a boxer?"

"Potato peeler."

"I've been to his restaurant. Your grandfather's much more than a potato peeler."

"It's an inside joke. He's the greatest."

"Understood. When you leave my office, you understand what phone call I'll be making, correct?"

Ray slightly rolls his eyes and sighs. "I understand, Father."

"Good. Go back to class now."

Ray stands and extends his hand. Father McDonald gives a paternal smile during their shake. Ray heads for the door.

"Ray, one last thing."

Ray stops and turns.

"How come you didn't punch Carlos in the face?"

"Because he's the new kid in school, and I didn't want him to walk around the halls with a shiner."

Father McDonald nods. "I'll take that under consideration when determining the length of your detention." He walks Ray out into a small entry area where his secretary sits. Once Ray leaves, he addresses her. "Please get Mrs. Ciancaglini on the phone."

. . .

Anthony, Bobby and Frank stand beside the garbage shed. They keep an eye out as trash flies out from it, accompanied by a loud rustling noise. Ray exits the structure. "Shit!"

"It wasn't there?" Bobby asks.

"No. Is her car still here?"

"Still here," answers Frank.

"Crap, school let out two hours ago," Ray says, frustrated. He takes a long hard look at the side entrance, then faces his friends with a mischievous grin.

"You're not thinking what I think you're thinking, are ya?" Bobby asks.

"I *are*."

"You got to be crazy," Anthony says. "You can't go in there and steal your magazine back. If you get caught, you'll be expelled. Christ's sake, you already got detention today for fighting."

"You got thirty-five cents you want to lend me? 'Cause that's how much *The Ring* costs."

"Hell no," Anthony responds.

"Then I'm going in. It's my magazine, so technically it won't be stealing."

"It was your magazine and technically *nothing*. Your ass is grass if you get caught."

"I won't get caught. I'm flying solo on this mission. You guys get out of here."

Ray enters the building, searches the garbage cans lined up

at the janitor's closet and, coming up empty, heads for Sister Saint Zita's classroom. He can see the lights are off behind the frosted glass window. Ray takes a deep breath, throws a one-two punch, then slowly cracks open the door to take a peek.

"Come in, come in, Ray," Sister Saint Zita says, sitting behind her desk with her shoes off and her feet propped up on her desk. Between her hands is Ray's boxing magazine. "What took you so long?"

"Uh, nothing."

"Oh, I thought it might be that you couldn't find your magazine in the dumpster, got impatient waiting for me to leave—knowing my car was still in the lot—and exercised an act of indiscretion by coming here to steal it back, thinking the classroom was empty because the light was off."

"*Um* . . . you're right, Sister. I'm sorry."

"Good. Straight talk is so refreshing, isn't it?"

"I guess so."

"Now sit your ass down."

Ray cocks his head back, surprised.

"What? You think it's okay to go around fighting and trespassing on school grounds, but a nun can't say 'ass?' Sit your ass down!"

Ray heads toward his assigned seat in the back.

"No, Ray. Up front. In Patti's seat. Maybe some of her common sense will sink in."

Ray complies.

"First, why in my class?"

"Because the geography textbook is the only one *The Ring* fits squarely into."

"Clever. You know you're only hurting yourself by not paying attention."

"I already know that stuff."

"Really? Name four American explorers in the textbook."

"Columbus, Balboa, Pizarro and Desoto. That was a gimme. They're *paisanos*. Want to know their routes?"

"Not necessary."

She holds back her smirk. "Ray, I always support student interests. In fact, I'm a boxing fan myself."

"I know."

"Really? How so?"

"The Basilio fight. The night he beat Sugar Ray. You were there in the restaurant, watching the fight with your father."

"Right you are. Anyway, your interest in boxing is leading you down a rocky road. It gave you the courage to take on Carlos and also led you here—now in deeper trouble. Father McDonald and I know how bright you are. Heck, not many kids would remember the face of a stranger in a crowded restaurant they saw during a fight when they were seven years old."

"Six."

"Six. But that's not the point. I'm concerned your intellect will go to waste if you continue boxing. Do you understand?"

"Yes, Sister. I understand."

"I'm not convinced. Not at all. But I said what I had to say. Now, if you bring *The Ring* into this building ever again, you'll be expelled. Understand?"

"Yes, Sister."

"And I'm giving you an additional three weeks' detention to the one week that Father McDonald gave you."

"Three more! That's not fair. Why three?"

"One for reading outside materials on my time. One for trespassing, attempting to steal back your magazine. And one to deter you from boxing."

"Man, doesn't seem fair since I only got one week for fighting."

"I don't believe in rewarding a student for bad behavior just because they spared another kid the humiliation of a punch in the face. Father McDonald and I don't always agree. Fighting is fighting, end of story. Thank you for giving me the opportunity to give you a punishment that fits the infraction. You may go now."

Ray looks at his magazine, still in the hands of Sister Saint Zita.

"You've got to be kidding me."

. . .

After spending the rest of the afternoon away from home—to avoid the wrath of his mother—Ray heads over to the restaurant. As he enters, standing there are Mom, Grandma and Grandpa— Mom with an angry look on her face and Grandpa with a pair of oven mitts in one hand, looking like he just got blasted with an earful.

"Where were you this afternoon?" Mom asks. "Never mind. It's not important. Now you listen, and you listen good. Never again. And you know what I mean. You have two strikes against you, and I suggest you don't strike out. Do you understand me, Ray?"

"Yes, Mom."

"Good. Forgetting about what trouble you're causing for yourself, you're tarnishing the good reputation of this family. I have to hear from Jenny Piccalo's mother in the supermarket about you beating up some boy who hardly speaks English, only to get home and receive not one but two calls from school. Your interest in boxing is a liability, Ray. A liability." She looks at the mitts in Grandpa's hand and then gives him a dagger stare. "And you're not helping either."

Mom walks out of the restaurant in a huff. Grandma gives Grandpa a disappointing look, then heads for the kitchen, leaving Ray and Grandpa standing there.

Ray looks at his grandfather with an apologetic expression

on his face. "Sorry, Grandpa. It's not like I go around picking fights."

"You might not pick 'em, but you sure as hell find 'em. You heard your mom. That's two strikes, kiddo. One more," he continues, shaking the mitts in Ray's face, "and we hang these up."

Ray nods.

"And tonight's training session is canceled." Grandpa walks away, leaving Ray standing there with his head down.

Comment: Ray Ciancaglini

That was a bad day. But I did learn my lesson. I stayed out of trouble for the next two years. The truth is, I never looked for a fight. Like Grandpa said, fights just found me. But I have to say, when they did, I was game. Especially when it involved a bully situation, which triggered my adrenaline. I believe boxers are born, not made. Like I said earlier, that's just how I'm programmed, and I own every bit of it inclusive of my diagnosis and life circumstance.

ROUND 4

Ray, age thirteen, and Anthony sit on a bench, joking around in Richard's Park. Behind them is Mrs. Marino, in her mid-seventies, hose-watering her garden, which abuts the park.

The boys' attention is caught by Jimmy Owens, a kid in their grade, who's running from a guy in his early twenties who means business. The guy catches Jimmy by his back collar and yanks him to a halt, ripping his shirt some. Jimmy, scared, turns, then pulls a few bills from his pocket, counting them out into the guy's hand.

Anthony gives Ray a look, like he should do something.

"I'm not getting involved, Anthony."

"Because of Officer Maloney?"

"Yeah. And my mom."

The guy violently shakes Jimmy, who now empties his other pocket.

Anthony gives Ray a second look.

Rolling his eyes, Ray stands, and he and Anthony briskly walk over.

The older guy turns and faces them in a not-so-friendly way. Ray looks at him and then to his friend, who is in obvious distress.

"What's going on, Jimmy?"

No answer.

Ray glances at the guy again. "Jimmy, do you owe him that money?"

Jimmy, nervous, looks at the older guy, then back to Ray. "No. I mean, yes. But not all of it."

The guy has his head cocked to the side, as if to say, *What are you going to do about it?*

"Why don't you keep what's yours," Ray says, addressing him, "and give Jimmy back what's his?"

The only response is an angry squint, elevating the already-thick tension.

Just then the faint sound of a squeaky faucet is heard, followed by the cessation of running water. A familiar voice comes from behind them. "Everything okay over there, boys?" It's Mrs. Marino.

"Everything's fine," says the guy, his glare still fixed on Ray. "I was just leaving." He looks at Anthony and Jimmy, sending them a smirk that says *my business is done here* as he walks away.

Mrs. Marino gives them a suspicious look, which is followed by another high-pitched squeak and the sound of running water.

Ray addresses Jimmy. "What was that all about?"

"I kinda, sorta owed that guy a few bucks from a bet he took. But he said I owed him interest and a collection fee."

"You better stop gambling. It cost my dad his job and landed him behind the bar at the restaurant. He's better than that and you're better than that."

. . .

It's evening. Mom walks to the foot of the stairs and calls up, "Dinner! Let's go. Everybody down. Now."

Five kids descend one after another and take their places at the kitchen table. It's an unusually quiet meal. Something is clearly bothering the parents. Just what it is will soon be revealed. As everyone clears their spot, Grandma and Grandpa walk through the front door. Grandpa is carrying a box. The grandchildren, surprised and happy, run over to greet them.

"Okay, everybody," Mom says, after several minutes, "now upstairs and do your homework." The kids begin heading up. "Ray, not you," Mom cautions. "Come into the living room for a second. Grandpa needs to talk to you."

Ray shrugs and enters the living room, curious. "What's going on?" he asks, looking at his parents and grandparents, all of whom are looking at him.

Grandpa hands him the box.

"What's this?"

"A gift."

"Thank you, Grandpa," Ray says, opening it. "What's this?"

"Exactly what it looks like," Grandpa responds. "A baseball mitt."

"I know that. What I mean is, why are you giving it to me? I don't play baseball."

"You do now. I had a talk with Coach Palermo of the Geneva Firemen's team, and he said you could join their thirteen-through-fifteen Babe Ruth team."

"But I don't want to be on their team. Heck, I don't want to play baseball."

"Don't swear in this home!" Mom yells, quickly changing the tone of things.

"I didn't. I said *heck*."

Mom turns to Ray's dad. "Angelo, do something!"

"Ray, your mother just thinks—"

"*We!* We just think!" She turns to Grandpa. "*We* just think. Right, Grandpa?"

"Yes, Irene dear." Grandpa takes over. "Ray, we—meaning all of us—think you should do something more productive with your athletic ability."

"But I don't like baseball. I'm happy training with you in the basement."

Grandpa raises his brow, communicating the sentiment that this was the last thing his grandson should've said.

"Just give it a try, Ray," Dad says. "It wasn't so long ago when you'd pretend to be Mickey Mantle when playing catch in the yard."

"I was like six years old. We were just fooling around. The kids on the firemen's team are real players. I can't play like them."

"You'll do just fine," Mom adds. "It will keep you out of trouble."

"I can keep myself out of trouble."

"Not according to Mrs. Marino."

"What's that supposed to mean? There was no trouble today."

"But there could've been. Baseball is a good wholesome game. And you were good at it in Little League."

"I'm not playing."

Mom looks to Grandpa. He reaches into the box Ray is holding and comes out with the baseball glove. "Sorry, Ray. But this is the only mitt you'll be putting your hand into from now on. Practice is at nine a.m. tomorrow at Shuron. *Capisci?*"

• • •

Sixteen uniformed kids occupy the baseball diamond at Shuron Field, some doubling up at the same position. Coach Palermo, in his mid-forties, is at home plate, hitting the ball as the team members respond with the appropriate play.

Ray arrives, wearing blue jeans and a white T-shirt, with mitt in hand. Coach Passalacqua, forty, large and overweight, stands in the on-deck circle and waves Ray over.

"Ray, my boy!" Passalacqua says. "Good to see you. Good to see you."

"Hi, Mr. Passalacqua. Good to see you again, too."

"*Coach* Passalacqua. Out here, it's *Coach* Passalacqua. In the restaurant, when I'm eating your grandmom's famous veal parm, it's *mister*." They share a smile.

"To be honest with you, I'm not sure about this," Ray says, his tone nervous. "I haven't played in a while. A long while."

"Don't worry. You'll do fine. Now go into that dugout and change into the uniform I left for you. Lucky number thirteen. Then head out to shortstop and rotate in with Nick."

Ray begins walking toward the dugout.

"Jog, Ray. We jog on and off the field."

Now in his uniform, Ray hustles out to shortstop, where his school friend Little Nick Navarino is in position. Ray is small for his age, but Little Nick is that much smaller.

"Hey, Ray. Good to see ya. What a surprise."

"You and me both, Nick. You and me both."

Coach Palermo tosses the ball. "Ray, coming right at you. Make the play to first." Palermo mishits the ball over the pitcher's mound. Ray darts toward second base, picking up the grounder behind the bag, then throws it to first. The ball sails over the first baseman's head and clears the fence, landing in the parking lot.

Coach Palermo turns to Passalacqua. "The kid's got speed, quickness and range. I'll give him that."

Passalacqua nods. "And you should taste his grandma's linguini in clam sauce, *marone*."

"Good get, Ray," Palermo yells. "Try to keep the throw down."

Ray nods.

"Here comes another one. Same play. And get down in the ready position this time . . . That's it." Palermo hits a line drive one-hopper directly at Ray. It pops up under his glove, hitting him in the crotch.

Ray goes down, cursing, holding his groin area.

Both coaches quick-step toward Ray. He's rolling around on the ground, holding his crotch. Every few feet, Passalacqua pulls up his baseball pants, which keep falling down over his giant-size behind. "Are you okay?" Palermo asks.

Sitting on his butt now, his head between his knees, Ray looks up, wincing. "I guess boxing ain't the only sport with low blows."

The coaches smile.

Ray finishes the practice, showing some promise.

Now, as the other kids head home, Ray is standing in the parking lot with Little Nick and the coaches.

"Sure, Ray," Passalacqua says, "you're a bit rusty, but nothing a little practice and your grandma's famous rigatoni a la vodka can't fix. Practice for you and the rigatoni for me."

Ray smiles. "Thanks, Coach. But I'm not sure baseball is for me."

"Your mom said we might be met with some resistance," Passalacqua responds. "But listen. Just give it a chance. Let's see how it goes. You're a solid hitter with strong hand-eye coordination. We just need to work on your fielding mechanics to get that throw down. It'll come."

Ray gives a reluctant nod, then turns to his friend. "Come on, Nick. Let's go."

Palermo puts up his hand. "Not so fast, Ray. We need to go over the league's code of conduct."

Ray nods.

"We expect good, clean, professional behavior both on and off the field."

"No problem, Coach."

"That means, no fighting."

"I only fight when I have to."

"Well, I expect that you won't 'have to' so long as you're on this team."

"But what if—"

"No buts about it. It's an absolute rule."

Ray nods and begins to head out with Nick.

"One last thing, Ray," Passalacqua adds.

Ray turns.

"If it's not too much to ask, could you see if your grandma can make that *fra diablo* tomato sauce tonight? Me and the missus are heading over, and, well, I know your grandma don't always have that on the menu specials."

"Sure thing, Coach. I'll ask her."

"Great. I just love it with her homemade pasta. See you two tomorrow, same time."

Ray and Nick begin their trek home with the coaches' eyes following. When out of earshot, Palermo turns to Passalacqua. "That kid's trouble."

"Naw, he's a good kid from a good family."

"Are you forgetting my sister's married to Officer Maloney?" Palermo reminds him.

"Naw, I ain't forgetting that."

"Well, I'm not sure it's in the best interests of this team to have a brawler around. You heard him with that 'what if.'"

. . .

Ray and Nick meander down the sidewalk. They pass the Variety Store, where Mr. Smaldone is sweeping the curb. Ahead, leaning against a building, are three twenty-something greasers, in leather jackets, two of them smoking.

"Shit. Greasers," Nick says.

"Just move to the edge of the sidewalk away from them and don't make eye contact," Rays responds. Nick does so with Ray moving behind him single file. As they pass, one greaser steps toward Nick and flips Nick's cap under the brim, knocking it off his head. Ray resists his impulses. As Nick bends to pick it up, the greaser shoves Nick off the curb into the street. He loses his balance and falls, his face hitting the asphalt. Bringing his head up he looks to Ray, scared, his face bloody. Putting his hand in his mouth, he comes out with a front tooth.

A different greaser—twice Ray's size—now moves to knock off Ray's cap. He's met with a swift, hard punch square to the nose, knocking him down. The greaser grabs his nose, now bleeding profusely. Ray turns to the other two, as if to say, *Who's next?*

Neither shows even remote interest.

Ray helps Nick up off the roadway. He then takes off his white T-shirt from under his uniform and hands it to Nick to hold against his mouth. They continue on silently.

Looking back, Ray sees the greaser still on the ground. Behind him, frozen with his broom in hand, is Mr. Smaldone.

■ ■ ■

The next morning the team, absent Little Nick Navarino, runs the bases, warming up. Both coaches are at home plate. Palermo yells, "Let's go! Let's go. Three-quarter speed. Three times around. Keep it moving. Keep it moving." Suddenly, his attention is distracted by a police car pulling up.

Maloney gets out and walks to the chain-link fence. Palermo turns to Passalacqua, "What do we have here?" Yelling to the players, who also seem distracted, he says, "You guys keep running until I say so. Bring it down to half speed."

The coaches walk over to Officer Maloney. "What's up, Sean?" Palermo starts. "My sister send you over here to harass me?"

"I wish that were the case," Maloney responds. "After practice yesterday one of your players assaulted a damn greaser. Put him in the hospital with a broken nose and a broken eye socket. You know how I hate greasers, but assault is assault."

Maloney looks past the coaches, scanning the players. "Ah, shit. Should've figured. Call Ray over here."

"Which Ray?" Passalacqua asks. "We got four."

"Ciancaglini. Who else?"

Palermo gives Passalacqua a disapproving nod. He turns toward the field. "Ciancaglini! Over here! Now!"

Having just rounded home plate, Ray jogs over, knowing the situation is not good. Maloney gives him the stare down as he pulls up. "Um, what's up, Coach?"

"Officer Maloney wants to have a word with you."

Ray looks to Maloney, separated by the fence.

"Son, you wouldn't happen to know anything about some greaser getting his nose busted yesterday, would ya?"

Ray hesitates. "No. *Um*, well . . . I mean . . ."

The Officer turns to his brother-in-law, Palermo. "How many number thirteens do you have on this team?"

All eyes are now on Ray.

"Officer, okay. You see? One of these guys roughed up Little Nick, and I, well . . . I just stood there and let it happen. You know, team code, no fighting. He got his front tooth knocked out because of me just standing there and doing nothing to help him. The guy was twice his size. But, when one of them came at me, it's like . . . I just hit him. You know? Without thinking, to defend myself."

"See? There ya go," Coach Passalacqua says matter-of-factly. "Self-defense. You can't hold that against the kid."

"No, we can't," Palermo responds, "but he just lied to an officer of the law by saying no when he knew it was yes." Turning to Ray. "You're benched for the first two games of the season for lying to the authorities."

Ray does not respond.

"Son," Officer Maloney begins, "what'd I tell you was gonna happen the next time I got word of you fighting?"

Again, no response.

"Go sit in the back of my patrol car. I'll spare you the embarrassment of cuffing you in front of your schoolmates and teammates. Go!"

Ray walks toward the fence exit.

"You're not really taking him in, are you?" Passalacqua asks.

"This kid would get six months in juvie if he got charged for even one of the fights he's been in. The thing is, not one altercation seemed to have ever been started by him. Just ended by him. And each for good reason, if there is such a thing as a *good* reason for fighting. He's the protector of the innocent, like some kind of vigilante. And he's never left the scene, either. Smaldone saw the whole thing. It went down just like Ray said. But he can't go around busting up people's faces. Even greasers. Broke his face with one punch. So, yeah, I'm taking him. Just where, now that's the question I'm struggling with."

. . .

Now sitting in the patrol car, the engine still off, Maloney looks in the rearview mirror, catching Ray's eye. "Seven."

"Seven what?"

"Fights. That's what my memo book says, and my memo book is never wrong. Most kids go their whole life without getting into even one scrap."

No response.

"And each fight was two hits, you hitting the guy and the guy hitting the ground."

Still no response from Ray.

Maloney turns the key, puts the car in gear and drives. Every so often he looks at Ray in the rearview mirror, struggling with his thoughts. After five minutes of driving in dead silence, the car now approaches the police precinct. Maloney checks his rearview mirror again, seeing Ray is clearly upset. He slows

down and pulls to the curb right in front of the official looking structure. He throws the car into Park, looks in the mirror
again, and then, just as fast, he puts the tranny in Drive and
pulls away from the curb, leaving the precinct behind them.

"Hey," Rays says. "What's going on? Where we going?"

Now it's Maloney's turn to give Ray the silent treatment. The
officer just keeps driving. It's not long before the official vehicle
pulls up to the bowling alley, where he puts the cruiser in Park.

Staring at the red neon sign, Ray asks, "Are we going bowling?"

"Not exactly. Get out," Maloney orders. "And follow me."

They enter to see several families occupying lanes one
through three on the left for a birthday party. The young girl
behind the shoe rental counter looks over to the manager, a
few feet away, as Maloney approaches with Ray trailing. "We
good?" Maloney asks the manager.

"Yeah, we're good."

"This way, Ray." Officer Maloney walks toward the first lane
on the left, then continues down a narrow walkway that runs
the length of the lane toward the pins. At the end of the lane
they make a right and walk behind the pin-set machines until
they arrive at a door on the left at the midway point that leads
to an area outside, behind the bowling alley, where a warehouse
stands. They approach and enter.

What's before them is a medium-size makeshift boxing training facility with young men in their late teens and early twenties
working out. Two rings are being used for sparring; off to the
side, guys are hitting heavy bags and speed bags, and boxers are
jumping rope nearby.

Ray's face lights up.

A muscular man, a trainer, approaches them, all smiles. The
bottom left corner of his lip is scarred and swollen. Permanently.

"Lip, this is the kid I was telling you about."

"Put out your hands," the trainer says. Ray complies. "Now turn them over. Make a fist for me. Give me a good firm handshake. He's got the right equipment, Sean. That's for sure. Wait 'til Monsignor gets a load of these mitts. What's your name?"

"Ray Ciancaglini."

"Ray Ciancaglini," Lip repeats. "If that ain't a boxer's name, nothing is. Heard a lot about ya, kid. All good."

Maloney shoots Lip a disapproving look.

"What I meant to say is, all good about your fighting, *uh* . . . sorry, boxing skills. But bad that you've been channeling them in the wrong direction."

Maloney nods as Ray turns to him for an explanation. "Son, if you want to fight, then this is the only place you can do it and not get in trouble. With me, that is."

"Um, Sean," Lip says, "we're shutting down this facility and we're bringing the fellas who train here over to the Buffalo Boys Town Gym. So if travel is a problem—"

"It's not a problem," Maloney responds without hesitation. He turns to Ray. "You use those hands pretty good, so do something constructive with them, if fighting is what's inside you. Can earn a pretty hefty living, too. One last thing. No more breaks. You're going to jail the next time you fight in the street. Do you understand me?"

"Yes, sir. But, Officer?"

"What?"

"My family doesn't want me to box."

"Yes, that's my understanding from Coach Palermo."

"No, what I mean is, they *really* don't want me to box."

"I know. The thing is, what's clear to me is that inside a gym is where you belong. I'll talk to your family. The Buffalo Boys Town Gym is a better alternative for you."

"Alternative from what?"

"Jail for aggravated assault."

Now evening, Ray stands in front of a pile of laundry on a table in the basement of the restaurant. Ray folds an apron and places it on top of other folded aprons. Grandpa comes down the stairs. Ray continues folding.

"Isn't this a twist of fate," Grandpa says on his approach.

"What?"

"We steer you away from boxing and onto the baseball field to keep you out of trouble, and baseball gets you into bigger trouble and back into boxing to keep you out of jail."

"It wasn't baseball. It was greasers."

"Whatever. Your mother almost had a heart attack when Maloney came by here. But I got to tell ya, he talked some sense into her. But then, the moment he left, she got all crazy again."

"She'll get over it," Ray responds.

"Oh, yeah? One time your grandma didn't talk to me for a whole six months."

"Really? What did you do wrong?"

Grandpa, about to answer, stops himself. "That's not important." Ray giggles.

"What about school?" Grandpa asks.

"I can do both."

"I have to admit that I am a little excited for you to be training at Boys Town with Monsignor Kelliher, but don't tell nobody. *Capisci?*"

Ray nods.

"When do you start trainin' . . . for real?

A smile fills Ray's face.

Comment: Ray Ciancaglini

Monsignor Franklin M. Kelliher was a well-known, retired Roman Catholic priest. He was also a boxing promoter and founder of the Buffalo Boys

Town—a home for troubled youth, homeless, paroled or otherwise. The proceeds from boxing helped support Boys Town.

Monsignor became a mentor and good friend. He showed great concern for my well-being, and I could count on him to tell me the truth, even if it was something I didn't want to hear. He taught me the importance of being a kind, considerate gentleman, despite the brutality of boxing.

ROUND 5

The Buffalo Boys Town Gym is nearly empty today. Some of the guys are off to an amateur-boxing tournament. Ray, who has now been training day in and day out for three months, approaches and stands next to Lip. They're watching two boxers spar. Monsignor is on the other side of the ring.

"That's Jessie Glover, right?" Ray whispers, leaning into Lip.

"Sure is."

"I read about him in *Ring*. They got high hopes for him."

"Sure do."

"I didn't know he trained here."

"First day. Monsignor persuaded Jessie to come over and try us out."

They continue watching the boxers spar. Jessie throws a hard body blow, and the clear *snap* of a rib-crack is heard. His sparring partner, Larry, doubles over, then falls to the canvas.

Monsignor steps through the ropes and approaches Larry, who is holding the left side of his rib cage. "Shit, you okay?"

"He broke my rib."

"How's your breathing?"

"Tough."

Monsignor waves over a trainer. "Get him to the hospital for an X-ray. There's always the possibility of a lung puncture with a broken rib. Get going. Now." The trainer helps Larry up and out of the ring.

Jessie, uninterested in the injury he has just inflicted, addresses Monsignor. "Who's next?"

"Today, nobody."

"What do you mean by that?"

"I had Larry here for you today. A lot of the guys and trainers are at a tournament. I'll try to get you a different sparring partner tomorrow."

"What do you mean, you'll try?" Jesse responds, annoyed.

"I can't just manufacture someone right now. I got to get the right guy to spar with you."

"You got me here to train, and the first day I got no one to spar with. You know I have a fight in two weeks. Every day counts."

"Let me get on the phone. Don't worry," Monsignor says, trying to calm him down. "I'll have someone here by this afternoon."

"But I'm training now!"

"I'll spar with ya, Mr. Glover," Ray says, looking up at them.

"I appreciate your eagerness, Ray," Monsignor responds, "but I can't even consider putting you in with Jessie."

"Why not?"

"Yeah. Why not?" Jessie adds. "The kid's game."

"You both know very well why not. Ray ain't ready for this yet."

"I'll take it easy on the kid."

"Yeah, he'll take it easy on me," Ray repeats without hesitation.

"You don't know how to take it easy, Jessie. Look what you did to Larry."

"Monsignor," Lip interjects, "mind if I talk to you for a sec?"

Monsignor steps out of the ring. He and Lip move to the

side for a private conference. "What's your great idea?" Monsignor asks.

"I know you've been busy and haven't had much time with Ray. But the kid has skills. He's been in the ring with some of the other guys and can hold his own. And given his history of street fighting—you know, taking on guys unable to handle themselves—well, maybe it wouldn't be such a bad idea to let Jessie take Ray down a notch. You know? Put Ray in his place, if you get my drift."

Monsignor gives a measured pause. "That may not be such a bad idea. But, if this kid gets hurt, it's on you." Monsignor looks up to Jessie. "We're going to let it happen. But take it easy on the kid. You got me?"

Jessie nods but lets a grin slip out.

Monsignor turns to Ray, who has an excited expression on his face. "You're getting what you asked for. Put on headgear and get in the ring."

Moments later, Ray steps into the ring and approaches Jessie, waiting for him there in the center. Ray puts his gloves out for a bump, saying, "Nice to meet you, Mr. Glover. A real honor. Thanks for the opportunity."

Jessie takes a step closer into Ray's personal space. "Keep your hands up and fight," he says in a low tone. "This is boxing. There's no such thing as taking it easy. Defend yourself at all times, or I'll knock out your ass. You understand me?"

"Sure I do," Ray responds with a whisper. "I guess you should defend yourself at all times, too." Ray raises his gloves for the customary bump.

Jessie smiles, then bumps Ray's gloves. They go to opposite corners as Monsignor and Lip look at each other in wonder at what was just said.

The bell rings. The boxers take center ring. Jessie throws a few jabs that Ray dodges. Jessie then throws a one-two combination, looking to take off Ray's head, which Ray also evades.

"Easy in there!" Monsignor says. He and Lip look tense.

Closing the gap, Jessie throws another hard one; Ray side-steps it and counters with a right uppercut to Jessie's chin, sending his head back and his body to the canvas.

Lip and Monsignor look at each other in amazement, with Monsignor commenting, "I take it back."

"Take what back?" Lip responds.

"He's ready."

Comment: Ray Ciancaglini

I was ready. Sure, I was just a kid from the lake trout capital of the world, but I had been preparing for my chance since I was six, trained by an old man sitting on a pickle barrel wearing pizza mitts. So Monsignor and Lip got me fights. In a short time I had ten wins and no losses, and people were taking notice. And my biggest challenge was next: Luther Johnson. He was undefeated, too, with nine wins in a row. All knockouts. Three of them were come-from-behind wins when Luther was badly hurt and on the verge of losing. Something, as I said earlier, that I had lost sight of on that one evening in Memorial Auditorium, Buffalo, New York. The evening when I sustained my *first impact*.

Let's pick up the count where we left off previously, during the Luther fight in June of 1967 . . .

ROUND 6

"Seven, eight, nine, ten." The ref waves his hands in the air, signaling the fight is over.

Ray, unsteady on his feet, wobbles toward the wrong corner.

The ref redirects him as Monsignor and Lip, now in the ring, give Ray congratulatory hugs.

"Attaboy, kid," Monsignor says.

Ray is slow to respond. "What happened?"

"What do you mean, what happened? You clobbered him." He turns to Lip, "The kid has the heart of a lion and the head of a jackass!"

"I won?"

"Stop playing games. Of course you won."

Ray looks to his right, having trouble bringing into focus what's in his field of vision. What he zeros in on are four empty front-row seats, then out of focus they fall. He looks around at the crowd. They are cheering and yelling, only Ray can't hear them. Like watching TV on mute. Then, a moment later, their cheers are deafening. As Ray leaves the ring, still unsteady, the applause becomes muffled. Confusion is plastered across Ray's face as he heads out of the auditorium toward the locker-room area.

. . .

Now alone in his dressing room, Ray sits on a wood chair,

hunched over, his forearms on his thighs, his head between his knees—in recovery mode. Two knocks on the door startle him; he's jumpy. "Yeah. Come in." The door cracks open. Ray's vision, at first double, brings into focus his visitor, Luther Johnson, now standing over him. As he looks up, Ray has no recollection of Johnson's approach.

"I thought I had you there," Johnson says.

"Me too," Ray responds.

"Then you knocked me clear into retirement."

"W-what are you t-talking about?" Ray struggles to get the words out. "That's your first loss."

"And last."

"Why? You quitting?"

"Morehouse College. Accepted today. Boxing was for tuition money. I'm going into politics. Effectuating change, equal rights. My people need to get a fair shake outside the ring. Listen. You got a couple reporters out there, waiting. Good luck, Ray." Luther turns and leaves as Ray watches the door shut.

Vision blurred, Ray struggles, finding a tape edge on his hand. He manages to lift the corner and unwraps his tape job. Slowly. Off balance, he steps into his pant leg, then loses his balance, falling into the lockers. It's a long while before he can fully dress himself.

Now leaving the dressing room, Ray approaches a small group of reporters at the hall's end.

"Hey, Ray," one begins, "you got a little lucky tonight."

"Ya know? You're right," Ray responds. "It seems the harder I train, the luckier I get." The group chuckles. "I gotta cut this short tonight fellas, you know, long drive home. One more question if you wouldn't mind."

"You took a hard hit in there, Ray. Will you be ready to fight next week?"

"See you in Syracuse."

• • •

Ray's lying in bed. His mom appears in the doorway, carrying a laundry basket. "Ray, you've been sleeping for two days straight. What's the matter?"

"Just tired, I guess. That's all."

She enters and pulls up a window shade.

"Geez, Mom. What are you doing?" Ray puts a pillow over his face, covering his eyes from the daylight.

"Time for you to get up and out." She takes the pillow off his face.

Ray slowly climbs out of bed, squinting.

"Come on. Let's go. Move it."

"I'm going. I'm going. Can you shut my door on the way out, please? I need to get dressed."

"Sure." She leaves. Just as the door closes, Ray lowers the shade and gets back into bed.

• • •

Later that afternoon, Ray enters the Boys Town Gym. He's met with congrats from boxers and trainers.

"Great job, Ray," says Len White, another young boxer and friend.

"Thanks, Len."

"I'm treating you to a victory lunch at the diner after training today."

"Okay, Len. That would be great. Thanks."

Soon Ray's hitting the heavy bag with Fred, an old-time trainer, who's holding it in place on the opposite side. Three fellows in their sixties, who hang around the gym, sit on a bench against the wall, watching Ray train.

Ray pulls up, wincing. "Ya know, Fred. I'm having bad headaches since the fight."

"Heard it before. Part of the game. Let's go. Keep punching."

Ray resumes hitting the heavy bag a few more minutes, then stops again. "These are kind of bad. You know. Like really bad."

"Like I said," Fred responds matter-of-factly, "part of the game. Let's go. You missed the last two days, and you have a fight on Saturday in Syracuse. We don't got time to waste."

Ray continues his training for several more minutes.

"Break," Fred says, then hands Ray a towel and a water bottle.

Ray sits down on the bench next to the three old-timers.

"Kid," the guy sitting next to Ray begins, "when you get hit in the head, you're gonna have headaches. Like Fred said, it's a part of this game. You have to deal with them."

Ray nods, understanding.

The guy on the end gets up and moves himself to the other side of Ray. "Son," he begins, "I've watched all your fights. Heck, I was here when you knocked out Jessie Glover. You have all the ability to get to the top. You can dish it out. We all know that. But, in this sport, you got to take it, too. If not, boxing ain't for you. Understand?"

Ray nods.

"Good. Now gut it up and work through these headaches."

"Work through them? How do you do that when you're getting punched in the head?"

The man finger-curls Ray in close for a whisper.

"That upsets my stomach," Ray responds.

Another finger curl and another whisper.

Ray nods at the advice.

. . .

Ray is in his dressing room at Syracuse Auditorium. Alone. He opens his locker, grabs his bag, reaches in and comes out with two small bottles. He throws back three pills from one and washes it down with a swig of Pepto-Bismol from the other. Just then, Lip enters with Monsignor and Ray quickly shoves the bottles back into his bag without them seeing.

Ten minutes later Lip finishes taping Ray's hands. He gloves him, pulls the laces taut and then ties them up. What Ray normally does at this moment is punch the gloves together to make sure they're on tight enough. But he doesn't.

"You all right?" Lip asks, seemingly acknowledging Ray's departure from the norm.

"Yeah. Why you asking?"

"Just asking, that's all."

Ray hops off the table, landing a bit off-balance.

Lip grabs him. "You sure you're all right?"

"Fine."

But Ray's expression says otherwise. Lip nods, then turns to Monsignor, raising a brow of concern. "Can I get a second alone, fellas? You know? With the big guy upstairs?"

"I guess now's as good a time as any for prayer," Monsignor responds with a smile. They leave.

Ray lowers his head into his gloves and closes his eyes. But it's not for prayer. His headache is splitting. Taking a deep breath, he stands, punches his gloves together, then exits the locker room.

. . .

Now in the ring warming up by dancing around and shaking out his arms, Ray listens as the announcer introduces the boxers. Ray raises his gloves up upon hearing his undefeated record with the crowd roaring in support. Now back in his corner just before the opening gong, he notes four empty front-row seats. Again.

The bell rings.

Ray comes out active, throwing a flurry of jabs. Yet within the first minute of the round he seems flat, lethargic, not as sharp as normal. By contrast, his opponent methodically throws lefts and rights, making Ray seem slow. He spends most of the round pinned against the ropes, eating hard body shots. Just before the bell Ray sees a left hook coming. As if in slow motion, he sees its course. Ray reacts to evade it, but with reflexes slower than normal, it slams him on the right side of his head behind his ear—in the exact spot Ray had taken Luther's left hook just seven days ago. Ray sees stars and wobbles off-balance, with his opponent loading his next punch. The bell rings, saving him.

Ray struggles to his corner and sits on a waiting stool. He looks up, expecting to see Monsignor. But instead the image he sees is the kind face of his grandpa. He's sitting on a pickle barrel, wearing pizza mitts.

"Ray," Grandpa says, "what'd I always tell you? Huh? Watch out for that left hook. *Capisci*? Ray, *capisci*?"

"*Capisci, capisci*," Rays says.

"*Capisci* what, Ray?" asks Monsignor, whose face now comes into focus, replacing Ray's disappearing grandfather's. "What the hell you talking about? Now come on. Look alive in there. You seem like you're in a fog. Look alive. Got me?"

Ray nods.

"And keep your guard up."

Another nod. "Bucket! Bucket!" Ray yells.

Lip ups the bucket.

Ray vomits a pinkish mixture into it. Monsignor takes note as Lip towels Ray's face with his other hand. The bell rings. Ray's up and out.

The next few rounds are brutal, each boxer connecting. Late in Round Four, while forced against the ropes, Ray takes a cutting shot to his right brow. Blood trickles, continuously. Ray gloves it away at every opportunity until the round ends. *Ding.*

The cut-man works on Ray's eye. Compressing, icing, swabbing. Still, the bleeding won't stop.

"Son, you're not listening to me," says Monsignor. "I said to keep your hands up. Now concentrate in there."

"Yeah, yeah, sorry."

Monsignor looks at Lip, as if to say, *What's going on here?*

The bell rings. Out goes Ray. He takes two quick jabs to his bleeding eye. The blood flows down his face, onto his chest and continues to his waist.

"Time out," the ref yells, getting between them and giving the appropriate hand signal. He looks at Ray's eye. "Doctor. Doctor!"

A doctor enters the ring and evaluates Ray's eye. What he sees is a small cut at the corner of his brow that just won't stop bleeding.

"I'm good. I'm good," Ray says, urging the doctor to continue the fight.

The doc turns to the ref. "He's good for now. Fight." The doc steps out of the ring. The ref hand-signals the boxers to resume fighting. The boxers box.

A few moments later, Ray takes another shot to the eye, spurting blood that won't stop.

"Time," calls the ref, signaling again for the doctor, who quickly steps into the ring and looks at Ray.

"This fight is over," the doc states.

The ref waves his hands calling the fight.

His opponent raises his arms in victory, while Ray punches his gloves together in frustration as he wobbles to his corner, blood continuing to flow.

■ ■ ■

Now in the dressing room, Monsignor and Lip are standing over Ray, who has a compress over his right eye. Ray looks up at them. "So I lost, right?"

Monsignor and Lip lock gazes, baffled.

"What kind of question is that?" Monsignor says. "Yeah, you lost. TKO. Bleeding."

"Right, right," Ray responds.

"*Right, right* is what you were taking all night. And lefts, too. And a big hook at that. What the hell? You got to keep your guard up."

Ray doesn't respond.

"I never seen a cut bleed like that," Lip adds. "Sorry, Ray. Our cut-man couldn't stop it. It's unexplainable, I'm telling ya. Ran clear down to your belt line. Just unexplainable."

Comment: Ray Ciancaglini

I can explain it. Those headaches that I'd been having over the last week . . . they were so bad that I had to take something. Every day. Four times a day. Aspirin—which is a blood thinner. And I took Pepto-Bismol because I can't stomach aspirin. Add to that caffeine and vitamin B pills for energy. I beat myself that night because it was a fight I never should've taken. I was suffering the continued effects of concussion. I threw away my whole career—and compromised my entire existence—for the sake of not missing one fight. This is the exact reason that this book was written—to prevent a second impact from ever happening to anyone else.

And that left hook I absorbed . . . it wasn't as hard as Luther's. But its impact was second-to-none. On my life. Yet I kept on boxing. It's part of the sport, right? Besides, a major amateur boxing tournament was just a few months away. You win that, well, you're *golden.*

ROUND 7

The sign on the outside of the Buffalo Arena reads Golden Gloves Tournament. Mounds of snow are everywhere around the front sidewalk from a recent storm. Inside there's a sign of a different kind. It reveals a ten-foot-tall single elimination bracket with the names of four boxers who've made it to the two semifinal fights. One of them reads Ray Ciancaglini, who's in the midst of the bout now.

"Off the ropes, Ray!" yells Monsignor. "Off the ropes!"

The boxers are in close. Their heads are banging during the bobbing and weaving. It's called dirty boxing. The bell ends Round Two of three. Ray drops down on his corner stool.

"You edged him out in the first, but he took the second. You need to reach deep, Ray. You got to go for the knockout in this last round. Don't leave it in the hands of the judges."

A blank look crosses Ray's face.

"You listening to me?"

"Yeah, yeah, finish him. I hear ya. I don't like this guy. He keeps head-butting me. And the ref's letting it happen. No warning, nothing."

"Just finish him," Monsignor says as the bell rings.

Ray goes across the ring after his opponent. He's got him on the ropes. Punches are exchanged. Ray catches the guy with a hard right, knocking him off-balance. Another hard right comes flying, knocking the guy to the canvas. Ray pounces down on his limp opponent, throwing another right, yelling, "And this is for the head-butting."

The ref reacts by pushing Ray off the guy, yelling at him to get to a neutral corner. Now standing over the downed boxer, the ref finishes counting him out.

Monsignor and Lip enter the ring, showering Ray with hugs. "Way to finish, Ray." Monsignor adds, "Way to finish. But you got to keep your composure in there."

The ref comes over. "You're lucky you knocked him out before he hit the ground, or I would've disqualified you. Keep it clean. You don't hit a man when he's down on the canvas, you know better than that."

. . .

After the fight, Ray and Monsignor go to Leo's Diner. Now in a booth, Ray sits across from Monsignor, who's gobbling down a plate of meatloaf and mash, while Ray eats hard-boiled eggs, one at a time. As Monsignor loads his fork, Ray, hearing giggles, glances to his right and sees Joe, a nineteen-year-old boxer Ray's become friendly with. He's in a booth with two attractive and playful blond girls.

"You ready?" Monsignor asks, bringing a heaping forkful up to his mouth.

"I'm ready."

"You don't seem ready."

"Well, I am. Why you saying that?"

Monsignor swallows his food, then leans forward. "This is the Golden Gloves, Ray. Upstate New York and Canada. The second largest tournament. I can't fault you for your performance because you're in the finals. But you seem a bit off. Lack of focus. You still getting those headaches?"

"They come and go. I told you that. The guys at the gym say

that's the way it is. So I'm just fighting through them."

Monsignor gives Ray a long stare.

More giggles come from the girls. Ray glances over. One smiles at him. Ray smiles back.

Monsignor seems annoyed at their interaction. "What was with you hitting that fella when he was down? You've never lost your composure like that. It could have cost you the whole tournament."

More distracting giggles from the girls. Ray glances over again. "I don't know. I mean, the guy kept head-butting me, and I just lost control. Lost my temper, like I can't stop it. Been happening a lot lately, you know? Like overreacting to stuff."

"What kind of stuff?"

"Stupid stuff."

"I'm listening. Like what?"

"Like the other day some guy swiped a parking spot I was about to pull into. Came from the other direction. I got out of my car and almost pummeled the guy."

"I hate when drivers do that, too. I get it."

"Yeah, well, there was another spot a few spaces away. So you know? It wasn't such a big deal. But I couldn't control my anger."

Monsignor cleans his plate with two big final bites. He pulls out the napkin stuffed in his collar as he stands to leave. "Okay then. You get a good night's sleep. Rest. Take it easy. And do the same thing tomorrow. The day after you fight for gold." Monsignor takes bills out of his pocket, tossing them on the table.

More giggles. Ray looks over.

Monsignor follows his line of sight. "You understand me, Ray? A good night's sleep. No extra curriculars. And let's keep tabs on this anger issue. That's quite unlike you." Monsignor leaves.

As Ray cracks his last egg, his attention is sidetracked by the infectious giggles again. Joe gestures for Ray to join them. Ray declines with a wave. Joe gets up and comes over.

"What's up, Ray? I need a wingman."

"You know I'm in the finals. I don't want to get distracted."

"That's the day after tomorrow. Tonight is tonight. You got all day to rest up."

"Still, Joe. It's the finals."

The girls prance over. Joe's lady friend, Nancy, an attractive eighteen-year-old, sits next to him. Jill, her gum-chewing friend who's a bit ditzy, parks it next to Ray, smiling at him.

"Ray," Joe says, "may I present to you the very beautiful and very available, Jill Malloy."

"Nice to meet you."

"You're cute. How come you didn't want to sit with us? Scared of a couple of college girls?"

Ray smiles.

Joe explains, "Because Ray over here is in the Golden Gloves finals, he doesn't want to get off-track."

"Well, I wouldn't get Ray off-track. I promise." Jill looks to Nancy, then snaps her gum. "Nancy, darling, have you ever known me to get anybody off-track?"

"I can't say that I have," Nancy responds, but their giggles say otherwise.

"What about you, Joe? Ever seen me derail anybody?"

"Can't say that I have. And I've known you now for almost three hours."

Jill looks to Ray. "There you have it. It's *ambiguous*. Now come along, Ray, and let's go out to play. Just a little. I'll be a good girl. I promise." Jill stands, pulling Ray's arm. Ray looks up. She cracks her gum. "Now come along. I promise that I'm not gonna hurt you. I nibble, but I don't bite. Okay, maybe I bite just a little."

. . .

The sign on the tavern reads Mickey's Bar and Grill. Flying out of the door come Jill and Nancy, stumbling, just a bit. Joe follows, then Ray.

"Make sure these girls get home safely, Joe."

"Home? Who said anything about home? The evening's young."

Ray gives Joe a look that says, *You know I got to chill.*

"Come on," Nancy says. "I got a surprise. Follow me."

Ray looks to Joe again.

"Just a little while longer," Joe whispers to Ray. "I really like this girl. And Jill is into you."

Ray looks at her, and a smile crosses her face.

"Come on! Follow me," Nancy says. They walk down the street and around the corner. "There it is."

"There what is?" responds Ray. "It's a big dark closed building."

"Closed to the public but not to me. And not just any building. It's the Buffalo Community Center." Nancy pulls a key out of her pocket and waves it about. "Come on. Side door entrance."

As Nancy slides the key in, Ray stares at the sign:

ABSOLUTELY NO ADMITTANCE AFTER HOURS.
VIOLATORS SHALL BE PROSECUTED FOR TRESPASS.

A tumbler click later, Nancy pulls open the door. Jill enters as Nancy turns to Ray and Joe. "Well, I can't hold this door open all night." They look at each other. Joe shrugs, then enters. "Well?" Nancy encourages. Ray enters hesitantly. "Come on," she says. "Time for a dip."

The four are now standing in near darkness at the edge of an Olympic-size pool. Nancy and Jill disrobe to their bras and underpants. Joe looks at Ray, smiling. The girls jump in and splash about, playfully.

"Well," Jill says in an alluring tone, "are you two just going to stand there or join the swim party?"

Just then the door they entered through swings open violently, and the beam of a flashlight shines in on them. It's in the hand of a police officer. "Stay right there," he orders, quick-stepping toward them.

Ray looks at Joe. They take off running toward an emergency exit, away from the officer who's now in pursuit. The girls watch from the pool, gum-snapping.

Once through the door, Ray and Joe run down the corridor toward a second emergency exit door next to a stairway. Without breaking stride, Ray depresses the release handle with one hand and pushes on the door glass with his other. It opens several inches, then abruptly stops, chained from the outside. Yet the forward motion of Ray's right hand pushes his palm through the glass and shatters it, pieces flying. "Shit!"

Behind them, the pool area door they exited through swings open. "Stop!" the officer yells.

Ray and Joe take their only option and run up the stairs with Ray's right hand leaving a trail of blood.

"Stop! Police!"

One flight up and through another door, they're out on the roof, scrambling around, looking for an escape route. But there is none.

The roof door swings open again and out comes the cop. With his flashlight shining on them, he approaches, walking.

Joe looks at Ray, then peers over the roof's edge.

"Stay right there!" yells the cop.

Stepping up, Joe jumps off the edge. Down he drops, landing in a ten-foot-high mound of snow. Ray looks back at the cop, then down to Joe, who waves him to jump. Off Ray leaps, landing in the soft mound. The cop looks down and watches Joe and Ray run up the street. As they turn the corner, the cop grins, knowingly.

"Stop right there!" A second police officer yells to the fleeing suspects, gun drawn.

Joe stops dead in his tracks, hands up. "Don't shoot!" he pleads.

Ray turns on a dime and continues to run.

"Stop! Or I'll shoot!" The officer is now aiming at Ray's back.

"Ray! Stop!" Joe screams. "He's got you! He's gonna shoot!"

Ray stops. His hands go up, his right profusely dripping blood.

. . .

Ray sits on the floor of a jail cell in Buffalo Police Station head-quarters. He hadn't slept a wink, partly due to self-recrimination and partly due to the community of unsavory fellows with whom he was forced to share the evening. He's holding his right hand in his left, the way someone does when injured. Two pairs of footsteps are heard approaching. Ray looks up. "Monsignor."

"Ray."

The officer takes out a ring of keys and unlocks the cell door. Ray gets up and walks past Monsignor with his head down. After completing the procedural requirements for release, they find themselves walking down the front steps of the police station. Silently.

At street level, Monsignor turns to Ray. "You're lucky I know a few people around this town. It didn't hurt any, that dame having a key to the building. Kind of hard to press charges for breaking and entering when a key gives access."

Ray smirks.

"Wipe that smile off your face. Now what's with your hand?"

"Nothing."

"Let me see it."

Ray slowly brings it up. It's coated with dried blood and an open laceration. "That needs stitches."

. . .

A few hours later, Ray and Monsignor exit the hospital emergency room, walk to the curb and stop, turning face-to-face. Ray's right hand is wrapped in a gauze bandage. "I expect this to be the last curbside talk that you and I ever have. Understand?"

Ray nods.

"You and I apparently have different definitions of resting, taking it easy and getting a good night's sleep."

Embarrassed, Ray does not respond.

"You beat yourself, Ray. The crazy thing is, you were the only one who could've beaten you in this tournament. Thirty stitches. And a wrist fracture. You forfeited the title match and all that you've worked toward. Jesus, I can't believe this. In all my years I've never seen such bad judgment be the waste of so much talent. You oughta have your head examined. Now, take it easy today, and I mean easy. Understand?"

"Yes, sir."

"I'll see you in the morning, like we discussed. Be on time."

Ray has no response. His defeated expression says it all.

Monsignor walks away.

Ray's left standing there, looking at the dirty snow gathered at the curb.

Comment: Ray Ciancaglini

Monsignor was right. I should've had my head examined. But it wouldn't have made much difference. By this time my condition was not only permanent but also progressive. And lack of judgment is a hallmark symptom of brain injury. As is my inability to inhibit my anger response. My capacity to plan was beginning to be off, too. It may sound silly, but just thinking about what time to get up, get ready, leave the house, and decide what route to take was also becoming an issue. The direction in which I was heading was at the point of no return, yet I had no grasp or understanding of this. At all. Again, a symptom of brain injury.

ROUND 8

Monsignor stands on the sidewalk, exactly where he had left Ray yesterday, with three large trash bags resting at his feet. Ray approaches lethargically. Monsignor glances at his watch.

"It's ten after eight. You're late."

"Sorry."

"After yesterday, *sorry* is not acceptable. We're talking ten minutes here. What's your excuse?"

"I don't have one." Ray looks at the bags, then at the building. "What are we doing here? I was hoping to avoid places like this moving forward."

"You'll find out soon enough. Let's go."

Monsignor, now wearing a Santa Claus costume, and Ray are in the children's wing of the hospital. One by one the kids hop on Monsignor's lap as Ray hands Santa toys from a garbage bag. By three o'clock they make their way back to the hospital lobby.

"Two things, Ray," Monsignor says as they stand by the entrance.

"What's that?"

"First, after the finals tonight, you'll receive the Golden Glove Heart Award, given to the boxer who showed the most heart, determination and resiliency throughout the year."

Ray's face lights up.

"The second thing is that lady approaching us in the hospital uniform is Dr. Friedman. She's a neurologist. I wasn't kidding when I said you should have your head examined."

A confused look crosses Ray's face. "*Um*, but I'm fine."

"Let's hope you are. Hey, Doc. Thanks for meeting us. This here is Ray, the boxer I was talking about."

She extends her hand. "Nice to meet you, Ray."

Ray shakes her hand while regarding this fiftyish, brown-haired, very professional-looking woman.

"Now, come with me," she says. Ray hesitates, looks to Monsignor, who nods, then he follows the doctor.

Monsignor watches as they make their way down the hall, turning into an exam room.

"Please put on this gown and hop onto the table. I'll be back in two minutes." As promised, Dr. Friedman reenters shortly thereafter with a clipboard in hand and sits in the guest chair. They share an awkward moment.

"Hey, Doc. I don't know why I'm here," Ray says, breaking the silence.

"Then I'll tell you. Monsignor asked me to see you because of your headaches. He also says that your judgment is off, that you sleep excessively, that you've showed inappropriate anger, that you're not following his instructions in the ring and, at times, that he finds you forgetful. Is he right?"

"Maybe."

"You're a senior in high school, correct?"

"Yes."

"How would you compare your grades from tenth to eleventh to twelfth grade?"

"Tenth and eleventh, with honors. Now . . . I'm struggling but just a bit."

"Were your grades better before you began competitively boxing?"

"Yes."

"And what do you attribute your scholastic decline to?"

"I guess I'm not putting enough time into schoolwork, that's all. You know, because of training."

"Are you not putting time into schoolwork because of training, or are you not putting time into schoolwork because you find the work more challenging since taking up boxing?"

"I guess a little bit of both."

"Tell me why the work's more challenging."

"I can't concentrate the way I used to."

"Anything else?"

"Things aren't sticking. It's like stuff comes into my head, then leaves right out."

"I see. I'm going to do a brief neurological screening exam on you." First, she checks his eyes with an ophthalmoscope. Then, making the letter *H* with her finger, says, "Follow my finger with your eyes. Get off the table and heel-to-toe walk for me, Ray." He performs perfectly. "Sit back down, close your eyes, and I want you to hold your arms out wide. Then, one at a time, bring them in and touch your nose." Again, done perfectly. "Cross your right leg over your left, so I can check your reflexes." She taps his knees. "Okay, then. We're done."

"How'd I do?"

"I couldn't elicit any abnormality."

"I told you that I was fine."

"We're going to do a test called an electroencephalogram."

"A what?"

"An EEG. It measures the electrical activity of your brain."

"I'm wondering why, if you just said my neurological exam was normal."

"Because it's medically indicated."

"Does it hurt?"

"No." Dr. Friedman applies multiple electrodes on Ray's scalp.

"Are you sure this won't hurt?"

"Positive. It tracks and records the electrical activity or wave patterns of your brain, that's all."

"Well, I hope I've got good patterns."

"Me too, Ray. Me too."

The test completed, Dr. Friedman says, "Get dressed and meet me in my office two doors down on the left."

Ray enters to see Dr. Friedman sitting at her desk with a furrowed brow and tracing strips between her hands.

She looks up as Ray sits opposite her.

"Well?"

"I don't believe in sugarcoating anything. These tracings are very irregular and highly abnormal. The—"

"How can I have a perfectly normal neurological exam but have an abnormal EEG?"

"You just can. It's not unusual. Now let me explain its medical significance in simple language. It means you need to pick another sport."

"That's not happening."

"I can only make medical recommendations. That's my first one. My second is that I'm prescribing Dilantin, an antiseizure medication."

Ray stands. "Boxing is my sport. And I've never had a seizure in my life. Heck, I've never even been knocked down for the count. You don't know what you're talking about."

"I do. I'm sending your EEG results to your doctor."

Ray walks out.

. . .

Inside the Boys Town Gym, Ray's working on the speed bag. But not just hitting it, giving it a beating.

"Holy crap," the mailman says as he passes with a stack of letters in hand.

At that, Ray gives the speed bag a giant whack, stops, and stares at him.

"Geez, man. Take it easy on that bag." The mailman continues on and enters Monsignor's office with Ray keeping a steady eye on him.

A few minutes later Monsignor sticks his head out the door. "Hey, Ray. Can I see you in my office please?"

"In a few minutes, okay? I got some rope training."

"Now, Ray. Now."

Ray tosses the jump rope to the side and heads for Monsignor's office. On his way, his friend Len, a fellow boxer, stops him.

"Is it true, Ray? You got a bout with Victor 'Tough Guy' Bush?"

Ray smiles proudly. "Sure is."

"You beat that guy, and you'll be right up there in the rankings."

"That's the plan, Len. That's the plan."

"Say, Ray—"

"Can ya give me a sec, Len? Monsignor wants me."

"Oh, sure, sure."

As Ray arrives at the door, the mailman leaves with an uncertain look on his face. Ray catches the expression, raising his curiosity, enters and sits. "What's up?"

Monsignor tosses a letter across his desk. The envelope is opened. "This came for you. Sorry, kid."

Ray looks at the letter, now resting on the corner of the desk. Then back to Monsignor.

"Read it."

Ray takes out two pieces of paper. The first is a copy of a letter Dr. Friedman sent to Ray's doctor concerning his condition. The second letter is on very official-looking letterhead. His brows furrow as his eyes move across the page. He slowly brings the letter down and catches the Monsignor's gaze. "This is horseshit!"

"Sorry, Ray."

"How did the boxing commission find out about my EEG?"

"Dr. Friedman."

"Can she do that?"

"She clearly can and did."

Ray tosses the letter and storms out. As he passes Len, heading for the gym exit, Len engages him.

"Hey, Ray, I was meaning to tell you that my brother's a trainer in South Carolina and Tough Guy trains in his gym. And let's say, there's no love lost between them. I can get my bro up here to help train you for the fight, if you want."

"There might not be a fight."

. . .

There's a crowd at Raymond's Italian Restaurant to watch the Friday Night Fights. The place is filled with energetic fans, except for one side table, away from the TV, occupied by Ray and Len.

"So the Boxing Commission says I can reapply once my EEG goes back to normal and if the medical advisory board approves me. They say to wait twelve to eighteen months."

"Twelve to eighteen months?" Len responds, in a tone of disbelief. "You're eighteen years old. You're entering your prime. You can't take off that kind of time if you want to be a contender. You know this sport. It's all about momentum."

"I know. I wish I knew what to do."

"Well, I sure as hell know."

Ray's mom approaches. Ray gives Len the sign—*mum's the word*.

"Gentlemen, are you enjoying your meals?"

"Yes, Mrs. C. Best pasta ever."

"Yeah, Ma. Thanks."

"So what are you two talking about that's so serious?"

"What do you mean?"

"What I mean, Ray . . . is you haven't missed a fight on that TV since you were six years old. That's what I mean."

"We're just going over some new training ideas. That's all."

"Yeah, new training ideas," Len repeats.

"I'm not convinced. Not at all." Angered, she turns and leaves.

"It's funny she's taking so much interest in my lack of interest in boxing, when she's never come to see me fight, not once."

"Yeah, I know."

"What do you mean, 'you know?'"

"We all know. Shit, man. You ask Monsignor for tickets to every one of your fights. He gets you four front-row seats, and, every fight, they're empty."

A disheartened look crosses Ray's face. "Yeah, when I see those empty seats during a fight, it's like a reminder, a message from my family that they want me to be a doctor or a lawyer. The first in the family to go to college. So they refuse to show support. Not even my grandfather has seen me box, and it all started with him. Anyway, go on. I'm listening. What were you talking about before? What should I do?"

"I told you about my brother in South Carolina. That's where you got to go. Keep fighting, just outside New York. The commission will never know."

"Can I do that?"

"Hell yeah, you can do that. Lots of guys go out of state when the commission pulls this shit."

"Really?"

"Yeah, really. Now listen. Just to make sure you don't have any problems down there or up here when you come back, you need to fight under a different name."

"What?"

"That's right. To ensure nobody finds out."

"But I'm gaining recognition, Len. Took a long time to get this far."

"Don't worry, man. You just take up an alias, win your matches, come back to New York, pass that brain test and start fighting here again. You'll make all the headlines. I can see it now. *Tony Hernandez, middleweight champ.*"

"Tony Hernandez? Who's that?"

"You."

Comment: Ray Ciancaglini

So I followed Len's advice. I went down south and fought under the alias of Tony Hernandez for my first bout and used different aliases in every fight thereafter. First to South Carolina, where I hooked up with Len's brother, but soon I found myself hopping from state to state—Mississippi, Louisiana, Florida, you name it, even crossing the border for several fights in Mexico. I was fighting one fight after the next, in mostly disgusting venues, arranged by scummy promoters.

Some of these states had no boxing commission, regulations or governing bodies at all. I got paid in cash and things went well. The competition wasn't all that great until I ventured into Mexico, where I faced high-level boxers. But it kept me in shape and in the mix. And I was feeling good. I stayed down south for more than two years, traveling from one venue to the next. But it was time to go back to New York for that repeat EEG. I was certain it would be normal. The only complaint I had was an occasional headache.

But headaches are a part of the game, right?

ROUND 9

Dr. Friedman walks into her exam room, chart in hand. "Hello, Ray. I'm glad to see you again."

"To be honest with you, Doc, I got a bone to pick with you."

"Oh, really. What's that?"

"You sent my EEG to the boxing commission, and they revoked my license."

"It's a relief to know they're doing their job."

"That's all you have to say?"

"Yes. I did send my report to them, and they did what was in your best interests. Now, why are you here?"

"I'm here for a repeat EEG. The commission's medical advisory board said I had to come back to you so you can compare it to the first one before I can get my license back."

"Yes, I'm familiar with their protocol. Okay. First, tell me what you've been doing over the last few years."

"Bowling."

"Bowling?"

"Yeah, bowling. You told me to find a different sport, right?"

She smiles. "You know the drill. We'll start with the same screening neuro exam and then repeat that EEG."

Ray nods, ready.

. . .

Ray is busy in his bedroom. It's decorated just like it was when he was a youngster. Only now he's ripping down the various boxing posters that have been up all these years. The only one he allows to remain is the Carmen Basilio versus Sugar Ray Robinson middleweight championship poster that had hung in the restaurant's window.

Next, Ray puts his awards, ribbons, trophies and the like—which fill the room—into several large cardboard boxes. Upon packing away the last one, he closes the box, turns, then punches a hole in the wall.

"What was that?" Mom screams from downstairs. "What the heck was that?" She swiftly climbs the stairs and enters Ray's room. Her jaw drops. The walls, dresser top and bookcase are barren, except for one poster. She sees the hole in the wall next to where he's standing. "Ray! What are you doing? For Christ's sake!"

Ray falls to his bed, putting a pillow over his head.

Mom sits down next to him, sensing how upset he is. She rubs her hand over his back. "Ray, turn over. What's the matter?"

Ray flips over, his eyes filled with tears.

"What's the matter, son?"

"I had this repeat test, Ma, to get my boxing license back."

"And?"

"And . . . here." He hands her a piece of paper from his bedside table.

She begins to read. "What's this all mean? All this medical language?"

"It means, I'm never gonna box again." Ray turns back around, burying his head in his pillow.

Mom looks up to the heavens and mouths, *Thank you.*

. . .

Ray walks toward Monsignor's office, stopping in the doorway. Monsignor looks up from his newspaper, and a giant smile covers his face. "Ray! Come in. Come in. Good to have you back."

"Good to be back," he responds, sitting across from Monsignor.

"Where have you been? I haven't gotten a phone call, letter, nothing for over two years."

"You saying you don't know where I've been?"

"I can't say that without getting into trouble with the big guy upstairs. I heard you—I mean, Tony Hernandez—were winning, fight after fight."

Ray smiles. "Yeah, I was winning."

"And now you came back, thinking you'd get your New York license, only to find out that things are worse."

"Dr. Friedman has a big mouth."

"She's only looking out for you, Ray. That's all. In fact, she's required to send her findings to the commission. Instead of resisting this, why don't we see if we can get you some real medical help?"

"Because I don't feel like I need medical help. I just lack some energy every so often and, you know, the headaches. What I need to do is box."

"Well, that's clearly not happening in New York. You'd have to go back to being Tony Hernandez or whoever and leave the state. And I'd strongly advise against that, given your medical condition. I'd suggest that now would be a good time to get down to the bottom of this. So, besides headaches and fatigue, what else is bothering you? Certainly, there must be something more."

Ray studies him. "Well, the only other thing is sometimes I feel like I'm living in a fog. And it upsets me, you know? Makes me sad."

"And you don't find that to be something that needs looking into?"

"Well, it's just . . ."

"Well, nothing. And that anger issue? You telling me that's over with?"

"No. I'm not telling you that. But . . ."

"But, nothing."

· · ·

As Ray approaches the large red-brick structure, he takes note of the physically and mentally compromised individuals sitting on benches, wandering around on foot, and wheel-chairing on the park-like property in front of the Clifton Springs Hospital & Clinic. Some have nurse aides by their sides.

"What the heck am I doing here?" Ray says under his breath as he enters the building.

"Can I help you?" asks the receptionist.

"I'm not sure I need the kind of help you're giving around here. At least I hope not, but I'm Ray Ciancaglini. I'm scheduled to be admitted for an evaluation."

"Oh, yes. Monsignor's friend."

Rays nods. "Yes, Monsignor's friend."

· · ·

Ten days after admission, Ray sits in Dr. David Singer's office, looking at the doctor's various diplomas and degrees displayed on one wall.

"So, Ray, you wanted to see me?"

"Yeah, Doc. About a few things. First, I really don't think I belong here."

"Yes, so you've shared. Repeatedly. And I've tried to impress upon you that denial of your condition is not uncommon in this setting."

"But I just don't fit in here."

"Ray, I appreciate why you would say that. But you have real clinical symptoms—headaches, lack of concentration, depression and problems regulating and inhibiting your temper."

"Yeah, but still. I'm functional. Not like the people being wheeled around in here."

"Okay, well add to that poor judgment—you fought down south when you were specifically told not to box after having your license suspended here in New York—which is what kept you on this slippery slope in the first place. Meaning, what's going on in your brain is preventing you from making good decisions. I've read your high school file. Lack of judgment was not one of your issues. In fact, just the opposite. You had a fight on the playground and didn't hit the kid in the face because you were concerned that others would make fun of him. To me, that is not just good judgment but a heightened sense of judgment, foresight and consideration for a kid you didn't even know and who came at you with a threat of violence. You're not that person anymore."

Ray lets his words go in one ear and out the other. "Doc, then there are these pills. I can't take them anymore."

"Why's that?"

"Because they make me feel like a zombie, that's why."

"Ray," Dr. Singer says in a measured tone, "you have to give your body time to adjust to the medication. You were admitted ten days ago, and you've only been on the meds for the last six of them."

"That's six days too long, if you ask me. I came here feeling foggy, and now I'm foggy, groggy and numb."

Dr. Singer takes a moment to make an entry in Ray's chart. "You're on a variety of antidepressants for severe depression. Your body will adjust, and, if it doesn't, then we'll adjust the dosage or switch to a different medication."

"And I don't get that, either. Sure, I'm down, but that's because I can't box anymore. Severe clinical depression though?"

"We verified with your mother that you were sleeping until nearly noon. And then she had to coax you to get out of bed. That is a classic symptom."

"With all due respect, Doc, I didn't need to come here for anyone to tell me that I was depressed. If someone told you that you couldn't practice medicine anymore, for no good reason, after investing your life in it, you'd be depressed, too."

"I agree. But your ban from boxing is for good reason. For your health and well-being. You don't want to get your arms around it—or better stated, you can't get your arms around it because of the injury to parts of your brain that are responsible for exercising good judgment—which is part of the reason why you're here."

"Well, I won't be here much longer. Which is to say, I'm leaving. Today. Now." Ray gets up and exits in a huff, closing the door firmly behind him.

Dr. Singer looks down at Ray's chart, makes an entry, then shakes his head, as if to say, *What a shame.* He closes the folder, picks up the phone and presses a button.

"Discharge coordinator," the woman says.

"This is Dr. Singer. I've been advised by Ray Ciancaglini that he intends to leave this instant. Please send a social worker to his room to try to talk him out of it."

• • •

Ray exits the front door of his home carrying a packed bag. Outside waiting are his parents and grandparents.

"Where are you going?" his mother asks.

"Away."

"Away where? You're not going back down south to fight, are you?"

"No. I'm not. It seems everybody is convinced my boxing career is over. Except for me, that is. But I will follow doctor's orders. It seems I lack good judgment."

"Ray," Grandpa says, "I'm so sorry this has happened. In a way, I feel responsible, encouraging you at such a young age." Tears gather in his eyes.

Ray puts down his bag and embraces him. "Don't be silly, Grandpa. Boxers are born, not made. I wouldn't trade our pickle-barrel training for anything in the world. No regrets. Besides, you always told me to watch out for that left hook, and I think that punch is what did me in. I love you." They embrace again. Ray now hugs his grandmother and father.

"I love you, son."

"I love you too, Dad." Ray now turns to his mother.

"Ray, please, where are you going?"

"I don't know. Just away. I need time to sort things out."

"You can't run from this, Ray. It will follow you."

"I know, Mom. I'm not running. I'm sorting, that's all." They engage in a long hug.

Mom reaches into her apron and comes out with a roll of bills. "Take this."

"That's not necessary. I made a good living boxing. I mean, how do you think I was able to afford this?" Ray nods to his Corvette convertible.

A tear trickles down her cheek.

Ray climbs into the Vette, sparks the engine, then looks up at her. "I love you, Ma."

"I love you, too."

Ray looks forward, puts the car in gear and drives away, leaving his family standing in the street. Wondering.

Comment: Ray Ciancaglini

I spent the following year mindlessly traveling around the country. But the Grand Canyon was where I found myself again. Where I was able to free myself from the thought that I couldn't get out of my head: my disbelief that, at age twenty-two, I had been confined to a mental hospital. Sure, I always felt that I was the last patient there who needed care. But clearly that thought was part and parcel of my injury. Just like the way I continued to box—in the face of an abnormal EEG. Because no rational person would ever have continued boxing.

Anyway, I learned that you can run but you can't hide. I knew what I had to do next in my life. I owed it to myself, and I owed it to my family. It was time to make my mother proud and come out battling, because that's what I do.

ROUND 10

Ray sits at the kitchen table, eating cereal. Mom walks in and hugs him from behind. "I'm so proud of you. Your first day of college. I always knew you'd go."

"Thanks, Ma. But I'm majoring in phys ed, that's all."

"That's fine. Just get your degree, then go to law school."

"But I don't want to be a lawyer. I want to be a phys ed teacher."

"A doctor is fine, too."

Ray rolls his eyes as Mom happily goes about her kitchen business.

. . .

Ray drives into the student parking lot at Monroe Community College, puts the Vette into Park and looks at the buildings. He's concerned and nervous. Walking to his first class, he realizes he's the oldest student on campus.

Now seated in the back row of a large lecture hall, Ray looks up at the buzzing and flickering florescent lighting fixture above; then his attention is caught by the instructor.

"Okay, class," the teacher says, "this course requires mandatory attendance. You will have an assigned seat, and, when it's empty, you'll be marked absent."

Ray tries to focus on the teacher's words, but the buzzing and flickering are distracting.

"You're permitted three absences. Then there'll be a problem after your third, unless you provide a reasonable excuse."

Ray puts his hands over his ears to muffle the noise and repeatedly looks at the light, squinting.

"Homework assignments must be turned in on a timely basis. No excuses," the teacher continues, as Ray closes his eyes and rests his pounding head in his hands. Now with the teacher's voice is sounding distant and garbled. "Are you okay?"

Ray looks up. The teacher is standing over him. The rest of the students have turned their eyes on him.

"Yes. Sorry. I was just distracted by the buzzing and flickering light," Ray says, pointing to the ceiling.

The teacher looks up. "There's nothing wrong with that light. And there's no buzzing."

Ray looks up. The light is working fine. He then looks at his classmates, who are still focused on him. "Oh, sorry," he says, embarrassed. "I'm a bit tired, that's all. I think maybe I should go."

"Well, if you're only tired, and you leave, that will count as your first absence."

"I understand. Sorry."

Ray gets up and walks out, feeling the eyes of the class following him. He heads directly for the school library, knowing what he has to do.

. . .

Now sitting in a private study room, Ray takes out and opens the textbook from the Health and Wellness class he has just left. The first assignment is to read a short passage and to answer the quiz questions. As he reads, the words come in and out of focus. He begins to use his finger, moving it across the page.

The more he reads, the greater the various challenges become. But he pushes on.

"There," he says, having finished reading three pages. Ray takes out a notepad and a pencil and begins to answer the multiple-choice questions at the chapter's end. "Done," he says. "Let's see," he whispers, "the answers are on page 247."

Ray turns to the back of the book and begins scoring the twenty questions. Dejection crosses his face as he continues marking the page. He closes the textbook upon completion and sits back in his chair, glaring at the notebook. He rips out the piece of paper from its spiral binder and leaves the graded paper on the desk as he stands and leaves.

The letter X dominates the left margin going down the page, with only a few check marks.

■ ■ ■

Later that evening Ray sits at the restaurant bar. The Friday Night Fights are on the new color TV. He eats slowly, watching the bout, disinterested. The atmosphere though, is fight-festive, as always.

Then into Raymond's Italian Restaurant walks Patti—twenty-four, blond, and bubbly. She sits at the bar next to Ray.

"Hi, Patti," says Ray's dad, tending the bar.

"Hi, Mr. Ciancaglini," she responds.

"How many times do I got to tell you, Patti? Call me Angelo."

"Sorry, Mr. Ciancaglini. I can't do that." She smiles.

"Suit yourself. Your food will be ready in ten. Sorry for the delay. As you can see, we're busy tonight, and the take-out orders are behind."

"That's perfectly fine." She turns to Ray. "Hi, Ray. Been a long time."

"Hi, Patti. Yes, it has. I think the last class we had together was with Sister Saint Zita."

"That's exactly right. And you didn't say two words to me throughout all of high school."

"Clearly, I wasn't very smart."

Patti smiles at his harmless flirt.

"And I'm even less smart now."

She ruffles her brows. "What's that supposed to mean?"

"Nothing. Sorry. Just a tough day."

"It meant something," Patti responds in a firm voice.

Ignoring her, Ray looks up at the TV. A boxer is hit with an uppercut and falls to the canvas.

"One, two, three," the ref begins his count. The boxer struggles to get up. He's dazed.

Ray yells at the TV, "Stay down. Stay down!"

Patti looks at the screen. "He'll lose if he stays down."

Ray turns to her. They lock gazes. "It might be for the best."

Just then Angelo places a small box filled with food on the counter.

Patti asks him, "Can you put this on my parents' tab, Mr. C?"

"Sure, Patti. Say hello for me. And get home quick. I don't want to hear your dad complain that the food was cold." They share a grin. Angelo turns to help another bar patron. Patti starts to pick up the box, but Ray intervenes, picking up the food for her.

Patti smiles. "Thanks. I'm parked just outside."

Ray follows her outside, opens the car door, and places the box on the front passenger seat. Patti gets in and leaves the driver's side door open as Ray comes around the back of the car. "Thanks, Ray," she says as he leans in. "See you around." She starts the car, then looks back at Ray. "Well? Are you going to close that door?"

"Patti . . ."

"Yes?"

"Do you think, maybe, well, do you think . . ."

"Ray Ciancaglini, are you trying to find the words to ask me out on a date?"

He gives a bashful grin. "Yes. Sometimes my brain has problems finding the words."

"Were you aware I had a crush on you all through high school?"

"*Um*, no."

"I didn't think so," she says in a cross tone. "And now you think you can ask me out on a date just because we happen to bump into each other?"

"Well . . ."

"And because you carried my parents' dinner to the car?"

"*Um* . . ."

"Is that what you think?"

A confused look crosses Ray's face. "Yeah, kinda."

Patti smiles. "Well, you're right. Do you know where I live?"

"Yeah, I know."

"Then pick me up at seven tomorrow night. You're free tomorrow night, aren't you?"

"Yeah. That would be great."

"Good. Now shut the door. I don't want my dad yelling at your dad because our dinner is cold. See you tomorrow. And don't be late."

. . .

The following evening Ray pulls up to Patti's house and parks at the curb. He gives the horn two quick beeps. Moments later, Patti exits the front door, looking beautiful, and gets in.

"Hi, Patti."

"Don't *Hi, Patti* me, Ray Ciancaglini."

"What? What? What'd I do? You haven't been in the car two seconds."

"You double-beeped me from the curb, that's what you did."

"So?"

"So any respectable young lady doesn't get double-beeped from the curb when she's being courted."

"So I'll beep once next time."

She tries to hold in her grin. "That's a bit presumptuous of you, isn't it?"

"What? What did I do wrong now?"

"You presume there'll be a second date. And we haven't even left the curb yet."

Ray nods. "You know what? You're right. If I have the honor of taking you out again, I'll come to the front door, ring the bell like a gentleman and escort you to my waiting chariot." Ray's smile is met by a reciprocating one.

"Now that's more like it."

Ray puts the car into first gear.

Patti grabs the shifter and pulls it down, back to Neutral.

"What? I couldn't possibly have done anything wrong by putting the car into gear."

"No, you didn't. But, before we go, I want you to tell me something."

"Sure, what?"

"What did you mean last night when you said you were 'less smart' now and your brain has 'trouble finding words?'" She gives him a prompting stare.

"Well, it's kind of difficult . . ."

"I thought it might be, which is one reason why I didn't press you last night."

"Oh, yeah? What was the other reason?"

"I didn't know whether you would show up tonight if I did, and I didn't want to risk that." Ray smiles. "But, since we're now officially on our first date, could you answer that question for me please?"

"Sure. You see? I was a boxer—"

"Everybody in town knows that, Ray. Father McDonald took great joy during Monday morning announcements, sharing your weekend victory over the loud speaker every time you won a fight. And my dad said you would be the next champ. So I'm well aware you were a boxer."

"Okay, take it easy on me."

"Sorry, go ahead."

"My brain ain't working right. From boxing."

"Maybe you got knocked out one too many times."

"That's the crazy thing. I've never been knocked out . . . or even knocked down. Not once. How do you explain that?"

"Ray, I really don't know. But I'm sorry. Not that this could make you feel any better or change things for you, but do you like live music?"

"Sure I do."

"Good." Patti takes two tickets from her purse. Ray's eyes light up. "There's this fella named Bruce Springsteen playing at the Smith Opera House in about an hour. Think this Corvette can get us there on time?" Ray's smile widens.

"I do believe it can." Ray puts the Vette in gear and rumbles away from the curb.

• • •

A young sombrero-wearing waiter collects the plates from the table. He reaches for the basket of chips.

"Leave those, please," Patti says. "And a little more guacamole, if you don't mind."

"More?" Ray questions. "You can pack it away for a trim girl, can't ya?"

"It's for you."

Ray smiles. "A girl after my own heart."

"That's right."

Ray's face lights up.

"And I just want to thank you again for taking me to the concert. Bruce was unreal tonight. But hey . . . wait a minute . . . was that part of your master plan to win my heart?"

"Maybe it was. Maybe it wasn't." They share a smile.

"Anyway," Patti says, picking up the conversation where they left off. "If you don't feel comfortable in college, that's perfectly understandable."

"It's tough. I'm not a quitter. I've never quit anything in my life. And it's not only that I don't feel comfortable, it's also *why* I don't feel comfortable."

Patti's nod urges him to continue.

"I'm not smart enough."

She leans back like she's surprised. "What? Sure you are. I know it was a long time ago, but you always came up with the right answers in Sister Saint Zita's class. I remember that specifically. Braun and brains. That's why I had a crush on you."

"That was then. I'm not that guy anymore. The first day I was excited to go to class, but once I was there, I started feeling out of sorts, so I just left. I went straight to the library to do my homework and to test myself to see if I was capable. The assignment was to read a short chapter on the nutritional importance of eating a proper and balanced diet for a health class. And I'm looking at the page, and I can't focus on the words. They're jumping around. And the more I tried to concentrate on them, the more my head pounded. Then finally I just couldn't concentrate at all, but I got through it. I took a multiple-choice test and I got most of the answers wrong. It's like I can't absorb new information. It goes in my head and then right out. And we're not talking about challenging material. And then there's my mom . . ." He pauses.

Patti puts her hands across the table, palms up. Ray looks at them as she wiggles her fingers. Ray places his hands in hers, and they look deeply into each other's eyes. "First, I'm sure there are therapies you can take to help with your reading and comprehension. You can improve, I'm sure. As for your mom, she will have to understand that your brain needs time to rest and to heal itself."

"That's the thing."

"What's the thing?"

"My mom doesn't really know the full extent of things. Neither does my father, or anyone else in my family. They know some, the little I've shared and what they've noticed for themselves, but not everything."

"Why have you been keeping it from them?"

Ray leans back. His hands slide out of and away from hers. "Why? I'll tell you why. I've never had any support from anyone in my family, except my grandfather. Every time I had a fight, I'd leave four tickets on the kitchen table, and not one time did anyone ever show up. I knew my grandpa wanted to, but he couldn't go against them."

"I want to say that's terrible, but maybe they just didn't want to see you brawling in the middle of the ring. I know I wouldn't want to see my son boxing."

"You have a son?"

"Not yet." Patti smiles as she says this to Ray. "But I hope to soon."

■ ■ ■

The menus scattered on the bar read "Felice's Watering Hole & Grill." Ray, behind a long wooden bar, is tending to patrons two rows deep. The crowd is eager to get their drinks, sliding in through tiny openings as people turn from the bar with drinks in hand. The other bartender, responsible for his half of the bar, serves three drinks for every one of Ray's. The manager, Billy, forty-five, watches from the corner. Next to him sits Patti, sipping her drink through a straw. Her focus is on Ray.

Ray points to his next patron.

"I'll have a vodka tonic. Very little tonic. Two limes and three olives on a stick. And in a wineglass, please, with very little ice. I mean, like no more than three cubes."

Ray stares at her, a bit confused. "A vodka tonic in a wineglass. You got it."

"Right. And don't forget two limes and three olives on a stick."

"Right. Two limes."

"And three olives on a stick. What's the matter? You deaf or something?"

Ray ignores her comment. He turns, reaching up for a highball glass and places it on the counter. Realizing his mistake, he puts it back and grabs a wineglass. He fills it with cubes and pours in vodka and tonic. He turns and leans toward the girl. "Two lime wedges, right?"

"Right. And don't forget three olives on a stick."

"Right."

She looks at the glass. "I told you three cubes. That glass is filled with ice. I know your play. More ice, less alcohol."

"Nah, I wouldn't do that. Don't worry. I'll fix you another." Ray spills out the drink and sets the glass on the bar.

At this moment a male patron leans over. "Excuse me? But can I get a drink over here?"

"Sure. One second. I'm helping another customer."

"Well, can you help her a little bit faster? We all need drinks over here," he gestures to the impatient patrons crowding the bar.

"Sure thing." Ray places three cubes in the glass, fills it with vodka and tonic, places two limes on the rim, turns and hands it to the girl.

"Where are my olives?"

"Right, olives. Sorry." Ray flips open the bar container, fishes out two olives, turns and tosses them in her glass.

"Really?" the young girl questions. "I wanted three olives on a stick, not two from your grimy fingers."

"Sorry about that," Ray says, unnerved. "The drink is on me." Annoyed, she grabs her glass and heads in Patti's direction, making a comment under her breath within Patti's earshot on the pass by. "That guy's an idiot."

A disco song begins playing, which excites the crowd, many of whom sing along. Across from the bar, in an open area, people begin dancing. A disco ball spins, its lights flickering across Ray's face as he addresses the young man anxious to place his order.

"Thanks for your patience. What'll you have?"

"I'll have a Bud, a vodka and cranberry, and a Long Island iced tea."

"What's in a Long Island iced tea?"

"I got no idea, buddy. You're the bartender." The customer turns to the girl he's with. "Hey, Nina. What's in a Long Island iced tea?"

"Tequila, vodka, white rum, triple sec, gin, lemon juice, some kind of syrup—I don't know what—with a splash of cola. And don't forget the lemon twist."

"You got that?"

"Yeah," Ray says, "I got it. Give me a minute."

Completely frazzled, Ray unties his apron, tossing it aside. He's now heading toward the rear of the bar. Billy, the manager, follows Ray through kitchen, out the open back door and into an alley, where Ray immediately leans against the building, eyes closed, frustrated.

"Is this your way of asking for a break?"

Ray opens his eyes. "Sorry, man. I really appreciate you giving me this opportunity, but this job isn't going to work out."

"Just give it some time. You'll get the hang of it."

"I can give it all the time in the world, but nothing's going to change."

"Why's that? Bartending ain't rocket science."

"Close your eyes for me, Billy."

"Really?"

"Yeah, really."

He complies.

"What do you see?"

"Nothing."

"And what do you hear?"

"Nothing."

"It's a peaceful place, right?"

"I guess."

"Well, as soon as I'm out of that peaceful, eyes-closed place—as soon as I open my eyes and find myself in an environment where things are happening—I feel overwhelmed. The lights, the noise, the people . . . Shit, Billy, just living moment-to-moment has become a challenge."

"I didn't know, man. What's going on?"

"I took a couple of hard hits boxing. And this guy asks for a Long Island iced tea in there, and his girlfriend barks out the ingredients, and I hear *vodka*, and I hear *tequila*, and then she goes on with the other ingredients, and it all just meshes together in my head. And I knew, if I went to make that drink, I'd be asking her—like three times—for the ingredients, and then I wouldn't remember if I put the vodka in first or whether it still needs it. And the music's blasting, the crowd is lively, and it ain't only the disco ball that's spinning. It's my head. I'm broken, man. I'm broken."

"Jesus, Ray, I don't know what to say."

"Say nothing. Don't tell no one. Especially my family. If it gets out, I'll never get a job, and I need a job, Billy. I need a job, a future, 'cause I met a girl, a real gem, and . . ."

"Yeah, Patti."

"How'd you know?"

"The way she looks at you, man. Listen. Just take it easy, Ray. Don't worry. I'm not telling nobody. And other jobs will be better for you. Don't worry. Don't worry."

Billy gives Ray a comforting rub on the back. "Listen. I gotta get back in there and help out behind the bar. You just take care of yourself."

As Billy turns to leave, Ray turns as well. Standing there just a few feet away in the doorframe is Patti. In her eyes are tears.

"*Uh*, hey, Patti," Billy says, walking past her. "Good to see you again."

She doesn't respond. But rather, takes two steps and she and Ray are face-to-face.

"How much did you hear?" Ray asks.

"Everything."

Ray rolls his eyes, upset.

"Don't worry," she says, closing in for an embrace. "We can make it together."

Comment: Ray Ciancaglini

My heart was broken, being unable to fulfill my dream of being a physical education teacher because of cognitive issues. But then another door opened that gave me hope and a life I could never have imagined or foreseen—behind that door was Patti.

Everybody should be so fortunate as to have a Patti in their life. I could not have lived mine without her. Here I was, twenty-four, unable to mix a drink, and she's not only telling me not to worry, she's saying we have a future. Thank you, Patti, I love you.

ROUND 11

From the outside, it looks like your typical starter home. Small, one level, old-fashioned, with curtains in the windows. Anyone could tell that the family who lives there gives it a lot of attention.

Inside, the place is sparsely decorated. Sitting at the small kitchen table with mismatched chairs is Ray and his daughter Anessa, now three and a half. Ray is drinking coffee, and Patti, who is eight-months pregnant, is standing at the stove.

Patti turns around with a pan of eggs in hand. She walks over to Ray and slides them onto his plate as he lovingly rubs her pregnancy bulge.

"Good morning in there, Little Ray."

Patti and Anessa smile. Placing the pan in the sink, Patti pours herself a cup of coffee and sits across from Ray while he gobbles down his eggs. "Are you ready?"

"Yeah. I can't live another day with you being the big bread-winner, supporting this family."

"I work because I want to, not because I have to. I love my job at the VA Medical Center. And you're raising a wonderful little girl and contributing with the money you make at the restaurant."

"But still."

"*But still* nothing. I put your sunglasses and earplugs in your lunch box next to your hard hat on the bench at the door."

"Thanks."

"Are you looking forward to this?"

"Very."

"You seem uneasy."

Ray swallows his last bite and puts down his fork, the way someone does just before giving an explanation. "Here's the thing. I can't waiter at my grandparents' restaurant anymore. They've been nice enough, taking me on, but I'm just not good at it. Getting orders mixed up, giving the wrong food to the wrong people, it's embarrassing. So, if this job today doesn't work out, I don't know what I'll do. And we got another little one on the way. I know you enjoy your work, but I don't feel like a man with the little money I contribute to this household. So if I seem uneasy, that's the reason why."

"I told you before we got married that we're a team. And we'll be just fine, whatever happens. We need to be thankful for what we have. And what we're going to have. We'll get by. And, as for you 'not feeling like a man,' there's not a guy out there manlier than you."

Ray smiles.

Patti moves close to him as he rests his head against her belly. Patti caresses his hair as Anessa gets off the chair and smothers them for a group hug.

. . .

Ray pulls into the lot, parks in between two pickup trucks, and gets out. Before taking another step, he stares at the construction site. It's an eight-story office building with framing nearly complete. The scaffold is partially constructed up to the second floor. "Here we go," Ray says to himself, putting on his hard hat as he approaches the office trailer, his lunch box in hand.

Standing there are two men in button-down shirts and hard

hats. One is Ray's childhood friend, Anthony. Resting on a construction-horse makeshift table are blueprints. Anthony looks up and sees Ray approaching. A big smile crosses his face as he waves Ray over.

"Ray! Get over here, buddy!" On arrival, Anthony hugs him and turns to the other guy. "John Armstrong, meet Ray Ciancaglini, my best buddy from childhood. The boxer I was telling you about."

"I heard a lot about you. Anthony goes on and on about how you protected the whole neighborhood when you were a kid."

"Anthony exaggerates. It wasn't the whole neighborhood."

"Pretty much was, Ray. Anyway, let's get down to business. Today will be a learning day for you. You know? Getting familiar with a construction site and our safety protocols. I'm assigning you to work with a team of laborers erecting that scaffold. Simple stuff, like Lego, if you know what I mean."

"Sure, Anthony. Whatever you want. And I really appreciate you giving me this opportunity."

"Think nothing of it. What could be better than working with my best and oldest friend?" They share a smile. "Come with me over to the fellas."

Ray finds himself standing with four laborers and Chuck, the foreman, at the base of a scaffold. At their feet is a stack of metal scaffold runner bars.

"Welcome aboard, Ray. Everyone here is excited to have you around."

"Thanks, Chuck. I appreciate the opportunity."

"Now rule number one is, safety first. Got it?"

"Got it."

"Great. Now, do you have any experience at all on a construction site?"

"None."

"Right." Chuck turns to the laborers fanned out around him. "You guys need to closely oversee and supervise Ray when I'm not in the immediate area. Got it?"

"Sure, we got it," one fellow says, as the others nod.

Chuck points to bars on the ground. "Ray, those are called runners. They're installed on and between the vertical bars across the entire exterior aspect of the scaffold. Their purpose is to keep laborers from falling off the edge."

Ray nods.

"That wheel up there"—Chuck now points to it—"is a hoist that lifts the runners up to the third floor, where we'll be working this morning. By noon, we should have close to all of them in place. Then we move up to the next floor."

Ray nods again.

"The procedure is, one guy down here loads the runners on the hoist. One guy up there operates it to bring the bars up. Then two other guys unload the runners and screw them into place between the vertical bars. One nut on each end of the runner and you got to screw it down tight. Understand?"

"Understood."

"You'll start down here, loading the hoist. Then, after a bit, I want you up there, operating the hoist. After that, before we break for lunch, I want you screwing in the runners with another laborer, so you taste a bit of everything. Got it?"

"Yes, sir."

"Good. Now let's get to work. I'll let you know when it's time to switch positions."

An hour later Chuck comes around. "Okay, fellas. Time to rotate. Ray up top and operate that hoist, just the way you saw Dave doing it."

"Yes, sir."

Ray works the hoist up top while two laborers remove the runners. Ray looks down to street level and the distance leaves him feeling a bit off-balance. He grabs a vertical, witnessed by Chuck and Anthony below.

"So, Chuck," Anthony says. "How's my boy doing up there?"

"So far, so good. Seems a bit uncomfortable with the elevation, but he'll be fine, once he gets used to it."

Anthony asks, "What are those big dark glasses he's wearing?"

"He brought them on-site. Says his eyes are sensitive to sunlight. The son of a bitch is as strong as an ox though."

Anthony nods.

The foreman looks at his watch. "Okay, fellas. Time to switch it up. Matt, I want you working with Ray, screwing on the runners. You're in charge of him, and make sure he does it right. You got me?"

"Got ya, boss."

The men go into motion, Ray and Matt now walking on the planking toward the hoist. They pick up a runner and walk it back to the verticals next to receive it.

"Okay, Ray. It's simple. First you unscrew the nut on the bolt that's welded to the vertical. Then put the nut in your front pocket so you don't drop it. Then you slip the eyehole on your end of the runner over the bolt, take the nut out, and screw it back on. Got it?"

"Got it."

They attach two runners with no problems. Now, picking up a third, they walk it to the next-in-line vertical, take off the bolts and slip on the runner. Matt, working faster than Ray, screws his nut on. As Ray's reaching in his pocket for the nut, a loud yell comes from above.

"Heads up below!"

A bucket of rivets comes showering down, barely missing Ray. A few impact the planking near his feet as the bucket makes a crash-landing at ground level.

"Everybody up there okay?" Chuck yells, with everybody but Ray responding yes.

"Ray?"

"Fine," he calls out. "Fine."

"Theo! What the hell is the matter with you? You got to be more careful. You could've killed somebody."

"Sorry, boss," he yells down. "It won't happen again."

"You damn right it won't happen again. Tie down your bucket!"

Matt, looking at Ray, sees his uneasiness. "You sure you're okay, Ray?"

"Yeah, I'm sure."

A whistle blows.

"Come on, then. Join me for lunch."

"Sure thing," Ray responds.

After their sandwiches, Ray and Matt pick up their runner detail where they left off. They carry a runner from the hoist to the next-in-line vertical and install it. "Give me a sec, will ya, Ray? That leftover meat loaf put a knot in my stomach."

"Sure," Ray responds, leaning against an iron girder of the building interior.

Matt leans against the runner they installed before lunch. "Holy shit!" He yells falling, with one leg dangling off the building's edge. The runner slides off the bolt.

Ray jumps forward, grabbing Matt's shirt and pulling him back onto the scaffold.

"What the fuck? What the fuck?" Matt yells. "The nut! The nut! There was no goddamn nut on that bolt to hold the runner on! That was you! Shit, man!"

Ray reaches into his pocket. He comes out with the large nut, revealing it in the palm of his hand to his co-worker.

. . .

"Don't be so hard on yourself," Patti says to Ray, sitting at their kitchen table. "Nobody got hurt."

"But I could've killed a man today."

"Well, those falling rivets could've killed you."

"That's not the point. I forgot to put the nut on. I was distracted for a second with those falling rivets, and then the whistle blew, and I completely forgot to replace the nut on the bolt to affix that runner."

"Well, you didn't have to quit."

"Yes. I did. I pose a danger to the other guys. A hazard. I appreciate your support. I'm going to bed."

Patti watches Ray walk out, dejected.

. . .

Ray pulls into the parking lot and looks at the giant sign. Eastman Kodak. "I better not mess this one up." He gets out and heads for the building.

Sitting opposite the desk of a bigwig executive, Ray says, "I appreciate this opportunity, Mr. Leonard."

"Certainly. Monsignor tells me a lot about you. All good. We'd love to have you here at Kodak, Ray, but the position we have open is one very few people want."

"Whatever it is, I'll take it. I'm thirty, haven't been able to hold a steady job outside my grandfather's restaurant, and I have a family to feed. I appreciate you doing this favor for Monsignor."

"It's no favor at all. We need to hire someone. It's hard to keep people in this position. Come on. I'll take you there." Leonard gets up, and Ray follows him out of the office.

Several minutes later they enter a giant-size, pitch-black, windowless space. Mr. Leonard flips on the light switch. "This is our largest darkroom. Where film is developed. You'll spend your entire day in here. Alone. In the dark. That's the first thing you need to know, and the reason why most people turn down this position. You sure you still want this job?"

Ray nods.

"Well, before you commit, why don't you sit in here for a while," Leonard says, guiding him to a stool at the film-developing station. "Just to see how you like it. I'll come back in a few minutes. And I won't be offended if you turn down the job."

Ray gives another nod then watches Mr. Leonard walk back to the door and open it. "You ready?" Leonard asks, now with his hand on the light switch.

"Ready."

Leonard flips the switch and the room becomes pitch black, except for the light entering through the open door from the hall. Now closing the door, Ray watches the light vanish. Complete and total darkness.

After a moment, tears gather in Ray's eyes.

Comment: Ray Ciancaglini

Those were tears of joy. Like Mr. Leonard said, most people would not want that job. But I'm not like most people. This was my dream job. Darkness. Quiet. Isolation. And a danger to no one. Including myself. I was at Kodak fourteen years and missed only three days of work. And for the last four years of my tenure there, I punched in every day at 6:15, skipped lunch and punched out early to avoid traffic on the road. I was a model employee.

However, near the end of my time there, the film researchers weren't so happy with me. I was unable to use the right chemicals in the right amounts for them to gather data on what combinations result in the development of the best film. But that's not why I was asked to leave. It was my trembling hand. The shaking prevented me from using the right amounts in mixtures, since it was difficult to release one drop when your hand's shaking.

And I was having problems following the proper chemical equations for a particular project, dropping carcinogenic chemicals onto the floor, and my film counts were off in the incubation department, causing them to have to repeat an entire research project. Twice. My job performance became unacceptable, despite many of my superiors covering up for me. The one thing you can't cover up is a positive sink test for mercury.

But that day in Mr. Leonard's office, sitting in the same seat he hired me in, was not where I was fired. In fact, I wasn't fired at all. He walked me to Human Resources, where they had already made arrangements at the University Medical Center for a disability evaluation. Now I wasn't comfortable receiving money for nothing, but I was educated to appreciate that disability benefits were developed to cover just this circumstance.

But that testing revealed my unfortunate destiny.

ROUND 12

CT scans are on a view box. Dr. Wilkens studies them. Ray and Patti watch. "So are you going to tell us what those films show?" Patti asks.

"A normal-appearing brain."

"So why am I shaking like this?" Ray holds out his arm.

"Because you have a brain injury. But these scans don't show it."

"Then why'd I have them?"

Dr. Wilkens sits back. "The community of thought is that your form of brain injury is microscopic in nature. That's the best answer I can give."

"It's 1995, Doc. You telling me that modern medicine can't show a brain injury on a scan?"

"A microscopic one, no. That's what I'm telling you. But the battery of neuropsychological tests I gave you over the last three days identified your preserved strengths and acquired weaknesses—concerning how you think, which is the cognitive portion, and how you feel, emotion, and act, which is the behavioral aspect. Preserved strengths are those domains that are just as good now as they were before your onset of symptoms. I can say with certainty that your math skills are the one category where I see full preservation. It's your acquired weaknesses associated with your brain injury that are problematic." Wilkens pauses.

"Go on," Ray says. "Don't pull any punches."

"Your ability to pay attention and your working memory have deficits. For example, if you're sitting at a red light, and it turns green, and you continue to just sit there, that means you're not paying attention. And, if you don't have good attention, you can't have a good memory."

Patti and Ray look at each other knowingly.

"Can I presume from that shared look that this has happened more than once?"

"Like once a week," Patti responds. "We're continually getting beeped at by other drivers, and we argue when Ray drives."

Wilkens nods. "Your ability to take in new information, to consolidate it, to put it into your memory so you can recall it at a later time has been compromised. This is the basis of your complaint of having difficulty learning new things. It's a factor of attention deficit and memory retention. Testing revealed your visual-perceptual and motor functioning—which is your ability to look at a task and to use your hands to coordinate the task—has reductions, which is part of the reason you kept spilling chemicals and dropping things at Kodak.

"Your information processing speed—how quickly the info you see or feel gets incorporated into the brain—also has reductions. Your executive functioning is severely compromised, which is one of the reasons why you were continually failing to properly complete your tasks at Kodak.

"Executive functions are necessary for goal-directed behavior. They include the ability to initiate and to stop actions, to monitor and to change behavior as needed, and to plan future behavior when faced with novel tasks and situations. Executive functions allow us to anticipate outcomes and to adapt to changing situations."

"Stop!" Ray yells. He puts his face in his hands.

Patti comforts him. "Just give him a moment, Doc."

"I'm sorry," Ray says. "It's a lot to take in all at once. A lot more than I expected, for sure."

"I understand," Dr. Wilkens says. "But *pull no punches* was my instruction."

"Yes, sorry. Please continue."

"Now, Patti, you had mentioned Ray is always getting lost on his way to new places, pulls to the side of the road and calls you for help. Am I correct on that?"

"Yes."

"Well, he's much like other men then, but, in his circumstances, it's because of this acquired deficit. Now, turning to how you feel—depressed—that's also been confirmed by testing."

"You didn't need to do any testing to confirm that."

"Yes, well, your mood and awareness, which is your ability to understand what has happened to you and how it impacts your daily functioning, is why you're depressed. You're aware that your functioning across many spectrums has been compromised, limiting you as a worker, a husband and a father. So you're depressed about it."

Ray sits quietly. Tears gather in Patti's eyes.

"Now taking all these things together, your history of repeated head trauma from boxing—"

"Doc, I'm telling ya that I took punishment like any other boxer, but I wouldn't call it repeated head trauma. I mean, there was this one week where—"

"Do you want me to finish?"

"Yeah, sorry. But it's just I wanted to mention the Buffalo-Syracuse week where—"

"Ray, let him finish."

"Okay," Wilkens continues, "the repeated head trauma, the findings on the electroencephalograms, my findings on the physical exam, plus the neuropsychological testing, leads me to the diagnosis of dementia pugilistica with features of anxiety, depression, headache, insomnia and global cognitive impairment. The shaking is Parkinson's syndrome, but you also have slowed gait with reduced arm swing disturbance, grade three upper extremity rigidity, and, well, the tremors that you already know about."

"You're making my head spin worse than it already does, Doc. Just let me know—let us know—what's going on? What's going to happen to me?"

Wilkens gives them the bearer-of-bad-news look. "These are progressive neurodegenerative diseases of the brain, which have no truly effective form of treatment, except for some mildly useful medications. I'm sorry, but it's a downward course from here. How quickly? Only time will tell."

"But I need to work. To provide. I'm forty-four, for God's sake."

"Ray, I appreciate you're a proud man. But you need to be on Social Security Disability. Kodak has already set this in motion on your behalf. And the report I will issue supports your disability application. So, no, you can't work any longer."

"I'll go nuts if I sit around all day."

"Volunteer your time somewhere. It will help you feel productive and useful. But working is out of the question."

Comment: Ray Ciancaglini

So that's what I did. Volunteer work. First with the Ontario County Probation Department, supervising community service for troubled youths. I was the guy on the grassy edge of State Route 96A with orange-jumpsuit-wearing youths holding litter pokers, picking up debris. I also tutored their schoolwork and tried to steer these kids in the right direction. I wrote completion letters to judges and felt a sense of accomplishment that I kept them from incarceration. I also spent time volunteer coaching pee-wee wrestling, doing some strength and conditioning training, and also coaching football and baseball at local high schools.

And while I did this, my angel Patti was the breadwinner. She had no problem with it, but I did. And always will.

But that Dr. Wilkens knew what he was talking about. My condition was progressive and began to limit my volunteering activities, until I finally had to give that up.

And my condition compromised my responsibilities as a father, too. I could give one hundred examples, but one in particular says it all. I went out for a walk one day, and then it hit me. I turned around and made it as fast as I could back to the house and up the stairs. I burst into the bathroom to find little Anessa and Ray Junior in the tub together, playing. They could've drowned in my absence.

My subsequent days were spent sitting in a rocking chair, looking out a window. Days turned into months, and months turned into years. And each morning when I woke up, I felt myself slip just a little bit more. It's a slow course, which I guess I should be thankful for. But I spent the better part of the next fifteen years unproductive. It's against my nature. It compounded my depression. It's no way to exist.

Now I only see doctors to adjust my medications, but I made an appointment with this one doc to make some plans. Permanent ones. Because the burden on my family is far worse than my living with this condition itself.

ROUND 13

Ray sits at the kitchen table, watching Patti ready herself for work. She pecks his cheek. "Bye-bye."

Ray heads for the front window, watches Patti drive away, then goes into motion, struggling to put his feet into his shoes. He grabs a set of car keys, pulls a piece of paper from his pocket, checks it, and enters the garage. He approaches the minivan, and the keys slip from his hand. He reaches down, hand shaking, struggling to pick them up. He gets in slowly and takes a deep breath. Starting the van, he puts it in Reverse and gives it some gas. *Bam!* "Crap!" he yells. He had slammed into the garage door, which he had forgotten to open.

. . .

Now arriving at his destination, Ray parks in the lot of a medical professional building. He opens the glove compartment and takes out a stack of three-by-five note cards bound by a rubber band, then anxiously heads for the building. "I'm here to see Dr. Harris," he says to the receptionist.

She pushes forward a clipboard with a pen attached. "Fill out the new patient questionnaire, please."

"That won't be necessary. I'm here for a consult."

"All new patients need to fill this out. We need your medical insurance information and—"

"Look. I'm paying cash. I mailed the doc my records, so she knows the answers to the questions on this sheet. If you could just let her know that I'm here, I'd really appreciate that."

"I'm sorry. But you must fill out this questionnaire. It's office policy."

Upset, Ray picks up the pen, hand trembling. He struggles to print his name when, from the back, in walks Dr. Harris.

"Is there a problem out here?"

"No," the receptionist begins. "It's just that . . ."

Harris looks at Ray's quivering hand, struggling to hold the pen.

"Mr. Ciancaglini?"

"Yes."

"No need to fill that out. But we'll need a copy of your license."

Ray nods.

"Follow me."

Now in an exam room, the doctor says, "Before we begin, I have a few questions for you, which will help me better understand what's going on." Ray nods. "I read your notes and reviewed your records. First, why did you want to see me so urgently? And why pay cash for this visit when you have insurance? Are you trying to avoid a paper trail? And stating three times in your letter not to tell your wife? I couldn't do that anyway, because of doctor-patient confidentiality, but clearly there is more to it than that. And not wanting me to send a consult note to your primary doctor, who I don't even know, but who you claim was the individual who recommended me? Mr. Ciancaglini, please help me understand. What's going on here?"

Ray has an emotional breakdown right then and there. The doctor waits for him to collect himself, which he does, then answers all of her questions in an hour-long back and forth.

"So you see, Doc," Ray says in a tone signaling the conclusion of a discussion, "I'm a boxer. Or was a boxer. But, once a boxer, always a boxer. It's your identity. And when you're a boxer, everybody has expectations. The same expectations you have of yourself. Which is to be the strong one—the fearless one. In command, never showing weakness. Regardless of the circumstances." He pauses a beat.

"And with my medical condition, I have no strength left. Nothing. And I don't know what to do. And I don't know where to turn. So, when I saw you on that TV show, talking about NFL football players and their brain injuries and how it impacts their lives and those around them . . . well, I knew I had to see you."

"I understand better now."

"I don't want anyone—my family, my friends, or even my doctors—to see me like this. My accomplishments and reputation as a boxer are what have kept me going. What's maintained others' respect. You know? . . . *There's Ray Ciancaglini, the boxer.*"

"I understand. May I speak?"

"Yes. Please."

"First, I understand your guilt about continuing to box outside of New York and against medical advice. And I understand why the long-term consequences of this decision have been difficult for you and why you think you've burdened your family. So, the initial thing you need to understand is that the way you feel is very common under the circumstances."

"That's relieving. But still . . ."

"Let's turn to why you continued boxing. If we understand the answer to that question, it will lead us in the right direction."

"Okay."

"You gave a very specific history of how this all began—in the Buffalo fight, when you sustained a concussion."

"But I didn't sustain a concussion. I wasn't even knocked out."

"You may not have been knocked out, but you did, in fact, sustain a concussion from that left hook to the head."

"How?"

"You don't need to be knocked out to sustain a concussion."

"Sure you do. What are you talking about?"

"I'll tell you. There was a misconception, in the days back when you were boxing, that you had to be knocked unconscious to sustain a concussion. Many boxers and other athletes believed that since they didn't lose consciousness, no brain injury was sustained. Thus, they went back to competing . . . prematurely. Then, while the brain was healing, some of these athletes were exposed to and received a second impact."

"The Syracuse fight?"

"Yes, the Syracuse fight in your case. One week later. You took another hard hit. We now know that when the brain sustains a subsequent impact during the healing phase from a prior concussion, the effects are devastating. Disastrous, really, because severe and rapid brain swelling occurs in those circumstances."

"This isn't sounding so good."

"Because it's not. But let's continue so you understand. In the most basic of terms, that first hit in Buffalo caused an acceleration force to your brain which sustained injury. In response to that trauma, there are various compensatory changes the brain goes through as it attempts to reduce this swelling. There are other metabolic changes also, defense mechanisms, all of which are the brain's way of reducing the potential for injury, that are beyond the scope of this conversation. Anyway, during the healing phase after this first impact, the brain is left vulnerable to the consequences of a second impact because these defense mechanisms, for lack of a better term, were nearly exhausted from the first impact.

"I don't get it. This is the first I'm hearing of this."

"Well, Ray, back then, the true devastation of sustaining a second impact while in the recovery phase of an initial concussion hadn't come to the attention of the medical community yet. Sure, it's common sense that you don't want a subsequent head trauma close in time to the first. But back then, the long-term consequences were not understood or recognized by the medical community. By the time you had your first EEG and were advised to stop boxing, the damage was done. That's clear from your records. Sure, continuing to box didn't help, but the long-term damage was done before that. In one week's time, with two hits, your fate was sealed. Your life situation is not your fault. You didn't know. Your trainers didn't know. Nobody knew."

"Two punches? Without being knocked out?"

"Yes. And because of this misconception—that you had to be knocked out to sustain a concussion—many boxers and other athletes where placed in, and put themselves in, harm's way. There was just no knowledge of the consequences of sustaining a second impact at that time. Had you known the potential consequences of your actions back then, which include chronic traumatic encephalopathy, dementia pugilistica and Parkinson's syndrome—you never would've taken that Syracuse fight."

"I'd like to think I wouldn't have. But I did have that abnormal EEG and continued to fight anyway—against medical advice."

"It was an abnormal test, yes. But nobody knew how devastating it really was in the guise of the increased risk of permanent brain injury from a second impact. You need to give yourself a break."

"It's just difficult to think I did this to myself."

"Unknowingly, Ray! Unknowingly! Then factor in lack of judgment being a symptom of the condition."

"But, still."

"Let's switch gears. You said in your notes that you've been living in a fog with continued physical decline, your depression is spiraling deeper and deeper, and there's no response to drug therapy, right?"

"Right."

"So, given your trials of medication, we need to accept that there's just nothing left to do medically. You need to accept that this is your life and continue to be brave."

"Brave I can be. And understanding that nobody knew how truly bad it was to sustain a second impact does give me some solace. So now can we talk about the other reason I'm here?"

"Yes, Ray. You want to discuss end-of-life issues."

"Right. I've stolen Patti's existence. I've been a burden on her. And I don't want things to end with her slaving over me once my independence is gone. And I especially don't want my kids to see me babbling, drooling and infirm. I can't have that, Doc. I just can't. And, most important, I don't want to linger on that way, without dignity. That's not how I want to be remembered."

"I understand, and that's not unreasonable. But the option you outlined—having someone drop you off at an out-of-state hospital with no identification so you can die anonymously and be buried pursuant to municipal law—is out of the question."

"But why? That insulates my family from my undignified end."

"You'll be depriving yourself of a proper burial. More important, you'll be denying your family the honor of remembering you and burying you ceremoniously, paying their last respects. Your family needs proper closure, and your ill-conceived plan will leave them forever wondering what happened to you. They may even spend the rest of their lives searching for an answer. Is this what you want for your family? Your children?"

"No. I don't. I guess I wasn't thinking."

"You were, just not rationally, part and parcel of your condition. And it's premature for you to consider end-of-life issues. Your condition has shown a slow progression. You could go on for two, three more decades. You may even stabilize at some point."

Ray nods. "It's just hard. I'm wasting away. Sitting in a rocker."

"So don't."

"But I can't do anything."

"Get outside. You don't need to do anything. Just get up and out. Share your story, so others don't fall victim to a similar fate."

"Share my story?"

"Yes. Share your story. Educate people about this. Educate teenagers, kids the age you were when this all happened."

. . .

"How was your day?" Patti asks, as she puffs up her pillow the way she always does right before resting her head down for the evening.

"Fine, just fine." Ray answers lying on his side, facing away from her, in sleep position

"Do anything special?" She asks, now on her side, facing away from him, eyes closed. Ray smirks, thinking about his visit to Dr. Harris.

"Yes, I did, actually."

"Oh really?" Patti questions, surprised at his response, which departs from the usual "no" answer. She turns toward him. "What's that?"

"I went to see a Dr. Harris who I saw talking on TV about football players and their head injuries." Patti pokes him in the back, he turns so they're face to face.

"Sure, I remember you telling me about her. But I didn't know you were going to see her."

"Well, it just kind of entered my mind, and she's not far from here, so I went."

"And?"

"And I learned all about the consequences of sustaining a second head injury while still recovering from a concussion." Patti's attention now locked in, Ray shares what he has learned.

"Good night, Ray. I'm happy you now know. You always did say those two hits were the ones that did you in. Now it's a fact. I love you."

"I love you too, Patti. Good night."

Ray closes his eyes, thinking about Dr. Harris's parting words—to share his story. As he falls asleep his mind begins filling with thoughts on how to prevent a similar fate from happening to another unknowing person. It's not long before he's in a deep sleep. The events of his day circling through his mind.

Ray's imagination puts him sitting front row in the bleachers with Patti at a crowded high school football game. The scoreboard shows it's the second quarter, with the home team winning 14–7. The quarterback marches the home team downfield to the two-yard line with repeated pass completions and skillful runs. The kid's father proudly yells from the stands, "Attaboy, Tommy. That's my boy!"

On the last play of the first half, Tommy bootlegs right and dives for the end zone. Airborne, he engages in a helmet-on-helmet impact, leaving him flat on his back, motionless in the end zone. The crowd goes from touchdown roar to complete silence. Tommy's father is frozen, staring, watching, waiting.

Two coaches run out on the playing field, and, after a motionless minute, Tommy is helped up and slowly escorted to the sideline. The crowd claps, and his father wears a relieved expression.

Ray's mind fast forwards the game to deep in the fourth quarter; the score is now 21–21, with Tommy on the bench the whole second half. The second-string quarterback is an inexperienced freshman who has been completely ineffective at moving the ball.

It's the last possession of the game, with the home team just having returned a punt all the way down to the five-yard line. The coach signals to Tommy, who puts on his helmet and heads out onto the field. The crowd yells with excitement at his return to play.

All except for Ray. He turns to Patti. "They can't put that kid back in. He was knocked unconscious."

"I agree, but he's on his way out there."

"I can't let this happen." Ray gets up and hurries as best he can down a few steps to field level, just as the coach calls a time out with his team now coming to the sideline to gather around him. Ray finally reaches the coach.

"You can't put that kid back in there," Ray says to him. The coach looks at Ray and cocks his head back.

"I don't need no punch-drunk boxer telling me how to coach my team."

This infuriates Ray. He now heads onto the field toward the referees, who themselves are now approaching him. They meet near midfield.

"What the hell are you doing, mister?" the younger ref asks.

"Saving a kid's life."

"Well, get the hell off the field, or I'll carry you off myself."

"I'd like to see you try."

The older ref leans into his partner, whispering in his ear.

"Oh, *uh*, listen, Mr. Ciancaglini," he says in a humbled tone. "I didn't mean you any disrespect. It's just that we've got a football game here to finish. So could you please get off the field, or I'll have no choice but to call the cops."

"Then call them."

Tommy's father now makes his way down and approaches the head coach. "What the hell is going on here?"

"That guy's a loon," the coach says, nodding out to Ray. "That's what's going on."

The refs are pleading with Ray to leave the field, now waving for the head coach to join them. He starts out onto the field with Tommy's father right behind him. The players stand on the sideline with their helmets off, confused, watching what's about to unfold. The crowd is booing, yelling at Ray to get off the field.

"You can't let your kid go back in," Ray says firmly to the father.

"Who the hell are you?"

"Who I am don't matter. It's who I was. I know what I'm talking about. Your kid was knocked out, and, if he takes another hit now, he could sustain a permanent brain injury."

The father turns toward the players, standing on the sideline, and sees Tommy with his helmet in hand. "What the hell are you talking about? He's fine."

"He may look fine, but he's not. He can't take a second impact before his brain heals from the first one. This one game is not worth a life-altering brain injury."

"But, Ray," Coach says, "if we win, we get home field advantage through the playoffs. I understand your concern, but the kid took a hit. That's all. He's not a boxer like yourself who took repeated head blows over a career."

"It only takes two hits, close in time, to do damage. I know what I'm talking about."

Tommy's father looks at the coach.

"Listen," the coach says to Tommy's dad. "I didn't want to say anything, but that guy up there in the front row, wearing an orange hat, is a college scout. He's here for your kid."

Tommy's dad looks over to the scout, then back to Ray and Coach. "He's my kid, and I say he plays. That's final."

Defeated, Ray walks off the field to a chorus of boos. He waves to Patti to come down from the stands, and they head for the exit as a whistle on the field blows to resume play. They stop and turn. The home team breaks from their huddle, and, as Tommy approaches the center for the snap, he veers off-balance, collapsing to the ground.

Whistles blow again, calling for the stoppage of play, and the refs motion the sideline for medical help.

Several hours later, Ray and Patti find themselves sitting in a hospital waiting area. There, with them, are Tommy's father and coach. A surgeon in scrubs with a mask around his neck enters and approaches. Tommy's father stands.

"Is my boy going to be all right?"

"He should be fine. The procedure went well. As discussed, I had to drill a tiny hole in his skull to drain the blood from a subdural hemorrhage compressing his brain. If you hadn't gotten here when you did, you could've lost him. In addition to the bleed he also has some brain swelling from the concussion. The bleed and swelling are a bad combination, but like I said, he should recover fully."

"Thanks, Doc."

"We'll admit him until he's stable to go home. I'll be in the hospital all evening. If you have any more questions, just have them page me." The surgeon leaves.

Tommy's father turns to Ray, "I owe you an apology. I was so caught up in the moment and the glory that I didn't even consider my own kid's well-being."

"I'm just happy he'll be okay."

"Me too. The thing is . . . he looked fine out there. Who knew?" The two men lock gazes.

"I knew." Ray nods, turns and leaves.

Ray and Patti are now approaching their car in the hospital lot. "Ray," comes a voice from behind them.

It's Coach.

He quick-steps up to them. "Ray, I owe you an apology, too. I'm really sorry. Especially for calling you punch-drunk."

"I understand. You were in the heat of competition. It's just that I had to learn this lesson the hard way—under the influence of that same competitive spirit."

"Well, I almost did, too. If not for you, things could've gone further south, and a young life could've been lost. And, I'm ashamed to say, it would've been all my fault."

"You didn't know. That's the thing with these injuries. They can be invisible. Tommy looked okay, standing over there on the sideline, ready to go in and to give his team their best chance at victory. That gave you and his father a false sense of security. But I know firsthand that the game you sit out today could be the career you save tomorrow."

"I'll tell you something, Ray. There's not one coach I know of who would've done anything different than I did today."

"That's the problem!" Ray yells out.

"What? What's the problem?" Patti, startled out of her sleep, responds to his yell with one of her own. "What's the problem, Ray?"

Ray, now awake, sits up.

"Ray, you were talking in your sleep. What's the problem? What are you talking about? You were having a nightmare." He turns to her.

"Actually, that was no nightmare at all. That was a moment of clarity. One of the few I've had in a long time."

"What are you talking about?"

"That dream was the growing seed that Dr. Harris planted in my brain. Now I know what I need to do."

Comment: Ray Ciancaglini

This fictional dream sequence was made a part of this work to illustrate a very realistic example of what goes on every day—innocent children being put at risk all for the sake of competition. Don't get me wrong, I believe in competition, but with safety protocols in place to protect head-injury victims. Today, concussion awareness is all over the news, finally becoming mainstream.

But because so few are aware of the dire consequences of sustaining a second impact while in recovery from an initial concussion, I started lecturing at high schools and then colleges, spreading the word about concussions and second impact. Before I knew it, I was booked as a speaker by institutions all over the country at banquets to raise money for concussion research.

But I realized I had to do more—reach a larger audience—before another kid sustained a senseless and otherwise preventable permanent brain injury out of ignorance: This situation needed regulation.

ROUND 14

New York State Senator Mike Nozzolio sits at his desk in Seneca Falls, his office filled with political memorabilia touting his accomplishments. Behind him are the American and New York State flags.

His door opens slowly.

In walks Ray.

"Mr. Ciancaglini," Senator Mike says, coming from behind his desk, his hand extended.

Ray reaches out—his arm shaking—Senator Mike taking notice. "Please call me Ray."

"Of course. Sit, sit. So, I read your letter. Very interesting. Very interesting. The name of this nonprofit you formed is The Second Impact?"

"Yes, sir."

"Now I understand what the consequences are from sustaining a second impact from your letter and also from having my intern do some research, but can you share with me the purpose of your nonprofit?"

"Sure, the point is, sustaining a second impact is completely and fully preventable; no child should ever be exposed to the risk of it. End of story."

"Yes, I agree with that. If the person who sustained a head trauma is not put in a position to sustain a second impact, further and more severe brain injury is preventable. And what is it exactly that you want me to do?"

"It's not what I want you to do. It's what you have to do. You need to prevent second impacts from ruining the lives of innocent children who don't know any better. The kids need to know, their coaches need to know, their parents need to know about the devastation of sustaining a second impact. So that the desire to compete and win doesn't place children in harm's way by exposing them to a second impact."

Senator Mike looks up, as if the answer were written on the ceiling. Then he looks back at Ray. "And how do you propose I do this?"

"By instituting a comprehensive law outlining a specific concussion protocol, mandatory for all schools to follow prior to a student returning to play after sustaining a concussion."

Senator Mike does not hesitate. "I'll do it. How does the Concussion-Management Awareness Act sound to you?"

A smile crosses Ray's face. "Perfect."

. . .

Ray stands in his bedroom, suit pants on, in the process of putting on his white oxford shirt. Patti, dressed for the event, buttons up Ray's shirt. She then slides a tie around his collar and makes a perfect knot. "Thanks," Rays says appreciatively.

"Sit down," she responds as Ray sits on the edge of their bed. Patti raises one foot at a time, puts on his socks and shoes, and ties his laces. Ray stands, and then she helps him put on his sports jacket. "You look the part, Mr. Courage."

They share a smile.

"Just let me check on my mom before we go." Ray's shaking hand picks up the home phone, and he dials. Two rings in, and she's on the line.

"What, Ray?"

"Is that how you say hello, Mom?"

"That's how I say hello to you when you're checking in on me for no good reason. I may be old, and I may be alone, but I can take care of myself. Now go to your event and make me proud." *Click*.

"Well, that went well," Ray says as he hangs up the phone.

...

Patti and Ray approach the front entrance of the Diplomat Banquet Hall, in Rochester, New York. The large sign proclaims the Twenty-First Annual Rochester Boxing Hall of Fame Banquet. They share an anticipatory smile and enter.

The crowded banquet room is filled with familiar faces, Ray's childhood friends, Sister Saint Zita, Officer Maloney, Little Nick, and countless others who Ray has touched in some way during the course of his life.

The honored guests are seated at long tables at the front of a stage, with a podium in the center. Notable guests include former World Champions Carmen Basilio, James "Quick" Tillis, Bobby Czyz, Charles Murray, plus former heavyweight contenders Ron Lyle and George Chuvalo. Ray has the honor of sitting next to Senator Mike and Assemblyman Kolb.

The master of ceremonies addresses the crowd by tapping the mic on the podium. "Thank you all for coming to the Twenty-First Annual Rochester Boxing Hall of Fame Banquet. Tonight, in addition to our boxing awards, we have a special presentation to kick off the festivities—the Executive Chamber Award. Senator Nozzolio, would you please make the presentation of the State of New York Resolution?"

Senator Mike approaches the podium with a rolled-up scroll in hand. Undoing the ribbon, he opens it and begins reading. "From time to time it is the sense of the New York State Legislative Body to recognize and to pay tribute to those exemplary individuals who have distinguished themselves through their outstanding commitment and who have attained the highest level of personal achievement. Thus, this Legislative Body is justly proud to honor Ray Ciancaglini.

"Ray was an aspiring boxer who showed great promise, moving up quickly in the boxing world. While Ray's reputation as a highly regarded boxer grew, so did his reputation for being a man of great character. At age sixteen, he was the recipient of the Golden Gloves Heart Award, an honor bestowed upon the boxer who demonstrates the most resiliency, tenacity and determination.

"Unfortunately, early on in his boxing career, Ray sustained two concussions close in time, which ultimately led to his diagnosis of dementia pugilistica and Parkinson's syndrome. These degenerative neurological disorders brought a premature end to his promising boxing career, which has been recognized by Ray's induction into the Geneva Sports Hall of Fame.

"Ray spent fourteen dedicated years at Eastman Kodak, retiring early due to complications with his diagnosis, complications he set out to prevent from happening to even one more individual. First, Ray helped pioneer the Professional Boxing Safety Act, which protects boxers from their own bad decisions by preventing a boxer with a license suspension for medical reasons in one state from 'state-hopping' and receiving a license to fight in a different state."

The crowd gives a round of applause. Senator Mike pauses. He continues as the clapping dies down.

"Then Ray committed himself to his heartfelt mission to help spread the word of the destructive nature of second-impact injuries and to continue in the fight to prevent adolescent and student athletes from being placed in the position of sustaining a second impact head trauma. Ray founded The Second Impact nonprofit organization, an educational concussion-awareness program aimed at educating student athletes on the repercussions of failing to address concussions properly."

Another round of applause, this time of higher volume.

"Ray uses his personal experience to raise awareness by educating young athletes about the possible dangers of sports-related head injuries by volunteering his time, and leading vital presentations and seminars at high schools and colleges. Ray was instrumental in getting the Concussion-Management Awareness Act passed into law, which sets out a protocol of treatment and evaluations to be followed once an athlete sustains a concussion, requiring physician clearance before returning to play."

More applause. Senator Mike nods over to Ray who gives a bashful smile.

"Whereas, it is the sense of the New York State Legislative Body that, when individuals of such noble aims and accomplishments are brought to our attention, they should be celebrated and recognized by all the citizens of the great State of New York.

"So it is resolved that this Legislative Body pause in its deliberations to honor Ray Ciancaglini upon the occasion of his receiving the Jerry Flynn Award tonight from the Rochester Boxing Hall of Fame. Thank you."

The room now erupts in applause. Senator Mike motions Ray over. They shake hands; then Senator Mike gives Ray a plaque and drapes a medal around his neck as the applauding crowd now rises to give Ray a standing ovation. Just at the right moment, the emcee steps in, and Senator Mike and Ray head back to their seats.

"Hey, Ray, we're not done with you yet," the emcee says. "Get back over here." The emcee, now standing behind the podium with Ray next to him, speaks. "It is with great honor that I present to you, Ray Ciancaglini, the Jerry Flynn Courage Award."

He hands Ray another plaque, and Ray holds it up, facing the audience, who now gives him a second standing ovation.

As the applause dies down, the emcee adds, "For those of you who haven't seen Ray speak, he'll be lecturing tomorrow at one p.m. at Belhurst Castle to the student bodies of both the Geneva High School and DeSales High School. All are welcome. Now it's time to turn our focus on the other honorees here tonight."

Comment: Ray Ciancaglini

That was one of the best evenings of my life. But now it's time to switch gears back to where this story began.

And then bring it home . . .

ROUND 15

"Ray! I said look at me!" Patti softly and slowly guides his face away from the loud-ticking green room wall clock. But not before Ray takes notice that he has relived his entire life over the last thirty seconds. They lock gazes. "You with us?"

"Always."

"Well, you had me fooled the way you were stuck on that clock for so long."

"The *tick* of a clock simply signifies the passage of time to most people. To me, as a boxer defined by rounds, it's that and much, much more."

"I understand. Now . . . are you ready to address those kids?"

"I am. Do me a favor. Call my mom please to check on her? She'll get mad if I call again, 'cause I called her last night. You know how she is."

"I'll call her. You take a sip of water." Patti picks up a bottle from the table next to the cheese platter, unscrews the top, and hands it to Ray. "You're on—"

"Ray, let's go! You're on," an usher's voice calls as the door swings open.

"Now." Patti says, finishing her sentence. "You're on now." They share a smile. "You go. I'll call Mom. Don't worry."

Ray nods and heads for the door.

"Are you ready?" Miss Hawkins, the Geneva High School principal, asks Ray, now standing at side stage.

"Sure. I used to get punched in the face for a living. This is no sweat."

Principal Hawkins smiles. They walk onstage as the high school kids continue to talk and text on their phones. They reach the podium, and Ray checks to make sure that the page-filled loose-leaf binder is secure on the stand as Hawkins addresses the students. As she speaks, Ray looks out over the sea of teens that fills the Belhurst Castle.

"Okay, students," Principal Hawkins says. "Let's have some quiet and your attention, please." The kids settle down, slowly. "Before we begin, everybody turn off your phone ringer. Come on, now." She waits a moment. "Okay, our guest speaker today, as you know, is Ray Ciancaglini. He has an important message to share with all of you. But especially with the student athletes. Mr. Ciancaglini, the mic is yours." She walks off the stage.

Ray sees the kids are all focused on him now. "Thank you for that kind introduction, Principal Hawkins." Ray takes a deep, calming breath. He looks down at his loose-leaf notebook, then back to the audience.

"I was a professional boxer. And, yes, it's a profession just like any other occupation. And every boxer knows the importance of having knowledgeable and dedicated people working in their corner. Although my corner now has new faces, their focus on my well-being is still their top priority, and I never let a day go by without thanking them for all that they do.

"My only regret as a boxer is that I didn't defeat my toughest opponent—in a fight I didn't even realize I was in. That opponent was a concussion, followed by a second one within one week's time. As a result, I've battled the effects of dementia pugilistica and Parkinson's syndrome for decades since.

"Today my condition also can be categorized as Chronic

Traumatic Encephalopathy, or CTE, a progressive neurological condition, which you might have heard about in the news lately, that many NFL players suffer from. Because of CTE, I've had a headache every day of my life since I was sixteen. My condition causes my hands to shake with tremors, has slowed my movements, leaves me off-balance and has compromised the way I think, how I feel, and the way I act, leaving me to live life in a fog. I can't even take an unsupervised walk with my grandchild because of memory lapses.

"My brain injury is the direct result of failing to properly address a concussion, something for which I take full responsibility and blame not a single soul, other than myself. Continuing to box, meaning getting back in the ring to fight, while still having the signs and symptoms of a concussion, was neither honorable nor courageous. It was a self-destructive act that cost me my quality of life and future potential.

"A concussion is an unpreventable risk of good, clean, hard athletic competition. But what is preventable is sustaining a second concussion before symptoms from the first one have been fully resolved. I am a living example that a second impact causes irreversible brain injury.

"I am here to share with you my life experience to prevent you from walking down the path of my life—a path of self-destruction. I learned that a concussion—with only mild symptoms—is the most deceptive and dangerous medical event you can experience. It gives you the false impression that it's not that serious. This misconception and the absence of visible signs of injury put you at a high risk for sustaining permanent brain damage from a second impact if you return to competition too soon. And, if you sustain this second hit to the head, well, I can tell you that your life will become a life of continual challenges, and coping with your loss of independence. Really, not a life at all.

"My CTE could have been avoided if I had known the

consequences of ignoring the red-flag warning of concussion symptoms. Simply stated, my error hinged upon a false notion that you had to be knocked out to sustain a concussion—something that never occurred during my boxing career. In fact, I had never even been knocked down. My story should serve as a deterrent for any athlete who might consider circumventing proper concussion protocol that we now have as state law.

"For those young people here today who have already sustained a concussion with continued symptoms, keep on punching toward recovery—but leave no doubt and wait it out before returning to competition.

"For the rest of you here today, my story began one evening in my grandfather's Italian restaurant when I was six years old . . ."

· · ·

Ray and Patti watch TV in their living room, sharing a large bowl of popcorn. "You did good today," Patti says. "Those kids were hanging on your every word."

"Thanks. I think it helped that there were a lot of athletes in that room."

"I'm sure it did. Anyway, happy anniversary."

"What? Oh, shoot! Did I forget our . . . wait a minute. It's not our anniversary."

Patti giggles. "It's your one-day anniversary since receiving your Courage Award. Happy anniversary, Mr. Jerry Flynn Courage Award recipient, with popcorn stuck on the corner of your mouth."

Ray smiles. "You like to tease me, don't you?"

"I sure do. Come on," Patti says, getting up and heading down the hall. "It's bedtime."

"I'll be in after a bit. I want to stay up for Saturday Night Live."

"Then you'll be up for a while."

"No, I won't. It's already eleven-fifteen."

"Yeah, but today's Friday." Patti disappears around the corner.

Ray picks up the phone and dials a number.

"The number you have dialed is out of service." *Wrong number*, thinks Ray. He dials again.

"Hello?" a man answers.

"Who is this?" Ray asks.

"You called me, man. Who is this?"

"This is Ray, Irene's son. Now who is this?"

"Nah, man. You got the wrong number." *Click.* The man hangs up.

Ray dials a third time. The phone rings until an answering machine picks up. "This is Irene. Leave a message at the beep." *Beep.*

"Mom, pick up. It's me, Ray. Pick up." Ray ends the call and dials again. The machine comes on again. "Mom. Pick up!" He waits. Nothing. Putting the phone down, he says to himself, "this is strange."

Ray walks into kitchen, grabs the minivan keys, quick-steps to the garage, gets into the vehicle and pulls his seat belt across his body. As he's about to engage it, he glances in the rearview mirror and sees a large popcorn particle in the corner of his mouth. He lets go of the seat belt, wipes away the popcorn, sticks the key in the ignition, starts the car, and puts it in reverse, forgetting to fasten his seat belt. He then backs out of the garage and down the driveway, running over the mailbox at the curb.

Patti, in bed reading, hears the loud bang and lays down her book the way someone does when listening for the second sound of a potential disturbance. "Ray? Is that you? What was that noise?" A moment passes. "Ray!" No response. Patti gets out of bed, puts on her robe and goes into the living room. The TV is still on and the couch is mysteriously empty.

"Ray! Where are you?" Nothing.

Patti enters the kitchen and immediately notices that the keys to the minivan are missing from their usual place. There, instead, is Ray's cell phone. Patti quick-steps to the garage door, hoping and praying to see the minivan behind it. She turns the knob, pulls, and . . . "Shit!"

Fast-walking back to the kitchen, she picks up the phone and dials. "Hello," Irene answers on the first ring.

"Hi Irene, it's me, Patti."

"Oh, I thought it was Ray again. I was just going to call him back."

"You didn't speak to him?"

"No. He called twice, but I was in the bathroom."

"This is just great," she says sarcastically. "I'm sure he's on his way over to check on you. Please call me when he gets there. I can't reach him. He left his cell phone on the counter for a change."

"He knows better than to drive at night."

"Yes, he does. Please call me when he gets there."

"I will." *Click.*

Patti goes into the living room and sits by the phone. Ten minutes pass, and it rings, startling her. "Hi, Irene. Put Ray on the phone."

"That's why I'm calling. He never showed up. Was he hungry?"

Just then the doorbell rings.

"I'll call you back." *Click.* Patti runs to the front door and opens it. Standing there are two state troopers with looks of concern across their faces. Behind them, parked at the curb, are their patrol cars, flashers on. She looks back at them.

"Oh, my God! Is he dead?"

"No. Critical," the trooper in command says. "He's been airlifted to SUNY Upstate Medical University Hospital in Syracuse."

"What happened?"

"Single-car accident. Left the road. Hit a tree head-on. He must have fallen asleep or been distracted."

"Will he make it?"

"The paramedics say it's fifty-fifty."

Her head drops.

. . .

Patti sits in the guest chair next to Ray's hospital bed. She's holding his hand. Lots of beeping is heard coming from the machines he's hooked up to. Ray's eyes open a slit, and he tilts his head in her direction. Glee appears on her face at his awakening. She gets up and moves in close.

Ray manages a few words. "What happened?"

"You hit a tree in the minivan."

"Last night?"

"No. Three weeks ago. You've been in a coma."

"Did I hurt anyone else?"

"No. Thank God."

"Am I paralyzed?"

"No."

"Why was I driving?"

"Going to check on your mom. Now's not the time for me to lecture you. But you know better."

"Yeah, I do." Ray pauses. "How bad am I?"

"You basically broke every bone in your body. No seat belt. They did surgery on your pelvis and ankle. You'll be here for a while. A few months of rehab, at least."

"Popcorn."

"Popcorn, what Ray?"

"That's the last thing I remember. Picking the popcorn out from the corner of my mouth." Patti smiles, then moves in for a cautious, but long, hug. As she releases Ray, they look into each other's eyes.

"I'm not ready," Ray says.

"Of course you're not ready. They won't start rehab for at least a few weeks."

"Not that."

"Not that? Then what? What are you not ready for?

"To make that donation."

Closing Comment: Ray Ciancaglini

Waking up, I knew I was in for a tough, grueling fight. I was hospitalized for thirty-three days and then confined to a chair for three months at home due to my broken and pinned pelvis and compound ankle fracture, which barely escaped amputation. But I kept my fighting spirit. The one thing in life we have complete control over is our attitude. Charles Swindoll said it best, "Life is ten percent what happens to us and ninety percent how we deal with it." And I dealt with it with Patti by my side and the overwhelming support of family and friends.

Closing Comment: Patti Ciancaglini

November 30, 2015, was the worst day of my life. Traveling fifty miles to the hospital, alone, in the dark, not knowing if I'd find Ray dead or alive, was an absolute nightmare. But each mile I traveled, I kept at the front of my mind that we're talking about Ray here. A true survivor. A lesser man in any regard never would've survived. And I'm not sure I could've made it through that evening had my brother Scott not been waiting there for me at the hospital when I arrived.

Through Ray's prolonged recovery period, he never complained, not once. I know Ray cherishes being given a second chance in life. And he's making the most of it with our three beautiful granddaughters, and with continuing his life's mission to educate young athletes and their families about concussion and the terrible consequences of sustaining a second impact. This is a man who has made the most out of an unfortunate life circumstance to the benefit of all.

Postscript

Ray is alive and well, living with his loving and supportive wife Patti in Romulus, New York, just south of his hometown of Geneva on Seneca Lake. He hopes his story will bring needed attention to concussion awareness and prevent student athletes from being exposed to the risks of a second impact to the head while recovering from an initial concussion.

The donation Ray referred to in the last sentence of this book is to a commitment he made to Boston University School of Medicine to donate his brain upon his demise for the further study of Chronic Traumatic Encephalopathy. Ray has been an integral part of the Legend study for CTE research at Boston University in life, and will continue to contribute upon death.

To all, Ray says, "Keep on punching."

Afterword
by Ray Ciancaglini

On Boxing: There are lucky punches. But luck has very little to do with success in boxing. It's all about ability, skill, smarts, dedication, perseverance and hard work.

On Life: I view life as an exact science. You get out of it exactly what you put into it. Your conduct will determine how you defined yourself and how others define you. Resiliency and determination defined my success as a boxer. It also defined my demise as a boxer and as an individual, something I didn't exactly bargain for or foresee. But I own it.

Pathophysiology of
Second Impact

In the most basic of terms, what happens with second impact is a second concussion occurs before a first concussion has properly healed. Even a mild concussion that occurs days or weeks after the initial head trauma can cause serious damage. Under this circumstance, the brain loses its ability to auto regulate intracranial and cerebral perfusion pressure. This may lead to rapid cerebral edema, which is severe swelling of the brain.

To be a bit more specific, secondary brain injury can develop in the days following the initial concussion, which creates ionic fluxes, acute metabolic changes, and cerebral blood flow alterations. All of these characteristics enhance the vulnerability of the brain, greatly increasing the risk of injury from a second impact of even less intensity than the first. Although rare, death has been reported to occur from cerebral edema followed by brain herniation in a matter of two to five minutes, usually without time to stabilize or to transport an athlete from the playing field to the hospital.

Most people now know about concussion protocol, to sit out and not to compete until the individual is recovered and symptom-free. This pathophysiology associated with a second impact is the reason why you sit out.

So now you know.

Acknowledgments
Ray and Patti Ciancaglini

Patti and I would like to acknowledge everyone who has shown us support, understanding and encouragement along the course of this challenging journey. The list of individuals is too long to mention by name. You know who you are, and we thank you for your kindness.

We would also like to acknowledge Andy Siegel. We first met Andy in Albany at an annual conference of the Brain Injury Association of New York State. When you are a survivor of traumatic brain injury, there is a certain "language" you speak, which is foreign to most. But Andy was fluent and understood our existence from the first instant. How comforting it was to finally meet someone who just knew. We are grateful that he shared our story in such a compelling and true-to-life manner. For that we say thank you.

And we are optimistic that with the publishing of this work, at least one life can be spared from being exposed to a second impact brain injury. Which makes it all worth it.

Acknowledgments
Andy Siegel

A giant thank you to Ray and Patti for giving me the opportunity to write Ray's life story. The brave way you both have taken on Ray's life situation is a lesson to us all. You both are champs! And an equally important lesson is the one taught by the message of this book—when your body and mind are telling you something is wrong . . . listen to them. Never expose yourself to the risk of a second impact to the head when in recovery from concussion.

As always, I would also like to thank my friends and family for their love and support. And I would like to acknowledge Patrick Nicholas for his creative input. Lastly, a big shout out to my numerous clients who have survived traumatic brain injury. You are champs too with equally compelling stories I have the unique opportunity to tell as your lawyer.

Ray's Scrapbook

Raymond's Italian Restaurant, Exchange Street, Geneva, New York, Established 1923

Interior of Raymond's Italian Restaurant

Ray's Mom

Ray's Dad behind the Bar at the Restaurant

Grandma and Grandpa in the bar at Raymond's Italian Restaurant;

Ray visiting his boxing inspiration, Two-Time World Champion
Carmen Basilio in Rochester, New York, who became a good friend.

Ray in 1966 at fourteen years old, weighing in at a trim 140 pounds

Monsignor Kelliher, Circa 1967

Chuck Jennings, Elmira, NY, at Neighborhood House Gym, 1967

Ray in 1969 at eighteen years old, weighing in at 156 pounds

Monsignor Kelliher in the Trophy Room at the Buffalo Boys Town

Ciancaglini in 156 class ——

Genevan wins Golden Gloves bout

BUFFALO, N.Y. (AP) — Seven Canadians and four Buffalonians were among the 15 winners Tuesday night as the regional Golden Gloves Boxing Tournament got under way.

The three round amateur bouts, for lighter weights, were the first in a series of three elimination blocks. The others will be held on Jan. 13 and 20. Semifinals will be held Feb. 10 and the title matches Feb. 27.

Tuesday night's results:

125

Ron Wilson, Buffalo, outpointed Justillano Morales, Buffalo.

Jon Mancini, Buffalo, outpointed Vernon Hubbard, Ithaca.

Doug Lane, St. Catharines, Ont., outpointed Ron Richardson, Buffalo.

Clyde Miller, Rochester, outpointed Allen Lane, Elliott Lake, Ont.

Tavo Mejia, Eden, outpointed Mike Byers, Buffalo.

132

Elijah Fields, Buffalo, outpointed Mike St. Pierre, Ajax, Ont.

Dan Stokes, Bay Ridge, Ont., won by TKO over Gary Dixon, Buffalo, 1:44 of second.

Boysie Ramkissoon, Toronto, Ont., outpointed John Beal, Oshawa, Ont.

Willie Ferguson, Kitchener, Ont., won by TKO over Ron Gonzalez, Binghamton, :56 of first.

139

Ian Platt, Simcoe, Ont., outpointed Hector Banza, Dunkirk.

147

Lenny Woodan, Rochester, outpointed Peter Russell, Lackawanna.

Yvon Richard, Kitchener, Ont., outpointed Bill Williams, Brantford, Ont.

Eric Bell, St. Catharines, Ont., outpointed Dusan Mucka, Hamilton, Ont.

156

Tony Mancini, Buffalo, outpointed Bob Murray, Binghamton.

Ray Ciangaglini, Geneva, outpointed Kevin Armstrong, Brantford, Ont.

May 20, 1970

CIANCAGLINI, Raymond A.

Dr. Bleakley:

I could not find any abnormality on neurological examination. The electro-encephalogram is a very irregular, relatively low voltage tracing without any clearly established basic frequency. There is some scattered slow activity at 4-5/sec. without any localization or lateralization. There is also a considerable amount of intermittent low voltage fast activity. Hyperventilation results in a buildup of the slow discharges and there are several paroxysms of irregular high voltage slow waves occurring synchronously in all the leads during this phase of the recording.

The patient's history certainly suggests a repeated head trauma and some concussion. I am actually surprised at the degree of abnormality of the electro-encephalogram, but this can probably be considered consistent with head trauma.

Neurological Consultation   CIANCAGLINI, Raymond A.
December 11, 1972

Neurological examination does not reveal any abnormality. Complete mental status examination not done. The patient appears to be somewhat slow in his mentation, but is fully oriented.

An electroencephalogram done today showed a very irregular tracing with a basic frequency of 8/sec. which was not well established. There is a great deal of scattered irregular slower activity. In the bipolar phase of the recording, there is some localized high voltage slowing in the occipital region bilaterally. There is also a great deal of high voltage slow activity at 2-3/sec. in the left temporal area and this is accentuated during hyperventilation. The tracing is grossly abnormal and consistent with cortical dysfunction. There is suggestion of left posterior abnormality.

The patient has probably had numerous injuries to his head.

An EEG records the electrical activity in one's brain. Ray's was abnormal. The findings are attributed to "repeated head trauma."

This is Ray's repeat EEG, after returning from his stint with underground boxing down south. Again, very abnormal.

Gramercy Gym ring in lower East Manhattan, 1971. Photo credit: Peter DePasquale

Al Galvin, renowned cutman and trainer at Gramercy Gym

Ray in 1972 at twenty-two years old, weighing in at 165 pounds

Ray and Monsignor with Al Galvin ready to pull the stool

Painting by Maureen McMahon

CLIFTON SPRINGS HOSPITAL & CLINIC
CLIFTON SPRINGS, N.Y. 14452

PATIENT'S NAME CIANCAGLINI RAYMOND

ADMISSION NO.	ROOM NO.	ADMISSION DATE	DISCHARGE DATE	TYPE CASE	NUMBER OF DAYS	PAGE NO.
735598-6	N-271	02/19/74		PSY	10	1
DOCTOR		GIMENEZ	MEDICAL RECORD NO.		BILLING DATE 02/28/74	

RESPONSIBLE PARTY NAME AND ADDRESS
MR RAYMOND CIANCAGLINI
383 N NORTH ST
GENEVA NY   14513   010

AGE	SEX	ACCOMMODATION
022Y	M	SEMI-PVT

FOR INFORMATION REGARDING THIS STATEMENT TELEPHONE (315) 412-9561

HOSPITAL SUMMARY

INSURANCE COMPANY -- BLUE CROSS   CERTIFICATE # 225060 CG5   GROUP #

DEPARTMENT SUMMARY	TOTAL AMOUNT	INS/COVERAGE	DUE/PATIENT
DAILY HOSPITAL SERVICE			
10 DAYS SEMI-PRIVATE	850.00	850.00	0.00
LABORATORY	22.00	22.00	0.00
MEDICAL - SURGICAL SUPPLIES	1.00	1.00	0.00
NEURODIAGNOSTIC LAB	50.00	50.00	0.00
OCCUPATIONAL THERAPY	5.00	5.00	0.00
PHARMACY	23.00	23.00	0.00
EMERGENCY ROOM DRUGS	1.23	1.23	0.00
HOSPITAL TOTAL	952.23	952.23	0.00

No person will ever understand what it feels like to be confined to a mental hospital for a condition that they can't even understand that they have. It was a living nightmare.

Committee Reports

103d Congress, 2nd Session

Senate Rept. 103-408

103 S. Rpt. 408

CORRUPTION IN PROFESSIONAL BOXING

SPONSOR: Mr. Glenn, from the Committee on Governmental Affairs submitted the following

REPORT together with ADDITIONAL VIEWS

TEXT:

At the same time, many states do a good job in properly regulating professional boxing events, and the Association of Boxing Commissions (ABC) has intensified its efforts to improve interstate cooperation regarding the standardization of rules, adequate health and safety precautions, and the sharing of information on bout results and suspensions. The ABC has wisely implemented a new policy of not recognizing the outcomes of boxing shows that have not been approved and supervised by state officials. This means that the boxers involved will receive no credit to their record for winning a bout, so promoters will have less incentive to hold shows without appropriate public oversight. This is the type of positive action that state officials and members of the boxing industry need to build upon to shut down the unsafe and fraudulent events that mar the sport.

The Professional Boxing Safety Act pertains to one of the penalties for State Hopping, which affected Ray. Ray never had any intention of claiming wins and losses for his alias's days, as that was a conscious effort to bypass the New York Boxing Commission, but to stay in boxing form in his intention to regain status in New York State, where he hoped to pass his second EEG test. In 1993, a staff member of Senator John McCain's office advised they had received his name and had solicited him to give information pertaining to the Professional Boxing Safety Act. Senators, working on the bill to stop corruption in professional boxing, contacted Ray. Ray was very reluctant at first and was then granted complete anonymity. Ray wanted to help because of what he went through and didn't want to see anyone else get hurt by usurping the law and state hopping. Ray agreed, with the stipulation that he would not give names, dates or places, but rather technical information. That way, the senators could understand the illegal practices going on in such a way to institute their efforts to bring it to a halt.

Ray with three-time World Boxing Champion Bobby Czyz at the 2011 Rochester Boxing Hall of Fame Twenty-First Awards Dinner Banquet. This special evening Ray was honored with receiving the Jerry Flynn Courage Award, being held by Bobby.

SENATOR MICHAEL F. NOZZOLIO
ASSEMBLYMAN BRIAN KOLB

**Honoring Raymond A. "Ray" Ciancaglini upon the occasion of his
designation as recipient of the 2011 Jerry Flynn Courage Award
by the Rochester Boxing Hall of Fame**

WHEREAS, It is the custom of this Legislative Body to recognize and pay just
tribute to those citizens who embody the true American spirit, demonstrating
personal courage and determination, and significantly contributing to the
enhancement of the quality of life of others; and

WHEREAS, This Legislative Body is justly proud to honor Raymond A. "Ray"
Ciancaglini upon the occasion of his designation as recipient of the 2011 Jerry
Flynn Courage Award by the Rochester Boxing Hall of Fame on Saturday,
November 5, 2011; and

WHEREAS, Born April 10, 1951, in Geneva, New York, Ray, was an aspiring
middleweight boxer from 1966 to 1972, who showed great promise of a successful
career; under the tutelage of legendary trainers and heavyweight champions, he was
extremely talented and moving up quickly in the boxing world; and

WHEREAS, While Ray's reputation as a highly regarded boxer grew, so did his
reputation for being a man of great character; in 1970, at the prestigious Niagara
District (New York/Canada) Golden Gloves Tournament, Ray was the proud
recipient of the Heart Award, an honor bestowed upon the boxer who demonstrates
the most resiliency, tenacity, and determination; and

WHEREAS, Unfortunately, early in his boxing career, Ray endured repeated head
trauma, a second-impact injury and was later diagnosed with Dementia Pugilistica,
a neurological disorder which often affects career boxers, and ultimately brought a
premature end to his promising career; and

WHEREAS, Ray then began a 14-year career at Eastman Kodak Company, where
he retired from early in 1994, due to complications from his diagnosis; Ray then
turned his sights to his heartfelt mission to help spread the word about the
destructive nature of second-impact injuries and to fight to prevent adolescent and
student athletes from suffering repeated head-trauma injuries in contact sports; and

WHEREAS, Ray has been called upon to contribute his time and talents to countless civic and charitable endeavors and he has always given of himself freely; and

WHEREAS, Dedicated and genuine, Ray is using his personal experiences in an attempt to raise awareness by educating young athletes about the possible dangers of sports related head injuries by volunteering his time leading vital presentations and seminars at high schools, colleges, and on the radio; and

WHEREAS, The founder of "The Second Impact," an educational concussion awareness program aimed at educating student athletes on the repercussions of not addressing concussions properly, Ray was also instrumental in getting "The Concussion Management Awareness Act" enacted into law; and

WHEREAS, Currently, Ray resides in Varick, New York, and serves as the strength and conditioning coach of the New York Collegiate Baseball League Geneva Red Wings Baseball Team; and

WHEREAS, Throughout his entire life, Ray has been involved in his community and Ray has stood constant in dignity, good grace and humor; and

WHEREAS, With him throughout his life have been his wife, Patti, of 31 years, and their children, Anessa (Ed) and Ray Jr., all of whom feel privileged to be a part of his life and rejoice in his achievements; and

WHEREAS, It is the sense of this Legislative Body that when individuals of such enduring courage and accomplishment are brought to our attention, it is appropriate to publicly proclaim and commend those individuals for the edification and emulation of others; now, therefore, be it

RESOLVED, That this Legislative Body pause in its deliberations to honor Raymond A. "Ray" Ciancaglini upon the occasion of his designation as the recipient of the 2011 Jerry Flynn Courage Award by the Rochester Boxing Hall of Fame; and be it further

RESOLVED, That a copy of this Resolution, suitably engrossed, be transmitted to Raymond A. Ciancaglini.

Signed this 5th day of November,
Two Thousand and Eleven

Senator, 54th District

State Assembly Minority Leader

Finally! Federal Law For Boxing

By DAVE ANDERSON
Published: June 29, 1997

IN other boxing eras, the names on the fight posters were enough to sell tickets: Ali-Frazier, Marciano-Walcott, Louis-Schmeling, Dempsey-Tunney. Now the big fights, like movies and plays, have marquee titles befitting their show-biz market.

For last night's rematch between Evander Holyfield and Mike Tyson - which Holyfield won in bizarre fashion when Tyson was disqualified after the third round for biting Holyfield in the ear - the marquee proclaimed, "The Sound and the Fury." For their original duke-out last November, it was "Finally!" - alluding to their five-year wait.

But now another boxing development deserves that "Finally!" title: a Federal law governing the sweet science that is too often sour.

On Tuesday, the Professional Boxing Safety Act takes effect. It is geared to protect the no-name boxers on small-time shows, rather than the pay-per-view champions, but it also could expose commissioners or promotors involved in what has become an ignored blight on boxing: conflict of interest.

It doesn't involve Federal control of boxing or a Federal commission. It' simply a hammer hanging over the heads of those who, up to now, couldn't be accused of breaking boxing's laws because there was no law.

It won't suddenly stop the corruption that too many people pass off with a shrug and say, "That's boxing." But it's a start. If diligently enforced, it would jail or fine those who have been able to hide by crawling back under the rocks whence they came.

"My concernd as public official are primarily focused on journeymen boxers," Senator John McCain, the Arizona Republican who spearheaded H.R. 4167, has said. "They strive to succeed despite their usually disadvantaged background."

In what has often been literally an outlaw world, journeymen boxers have sometimes fought without state-to-state medical supervision, sometimes under assumed names, sometimes in states without a commission.

Now a professional boxer must register with a state commission, be issued an identification card and be asigned a number by a boxing registry. Each commission shall evaluate a boxer's ring record, medical records, recent knockout losses, consecutive losses.

Results of all professional boxing matches must now be reported to boxing registries within 48 hours.

Under the new law, standards for safety include health insurance for each boxer as well as a physical exam, a ringside physician and an ambulance or medical personnel with resuscitation equipment on site.

That might sound like what some commissions have been doing, anyway, but not all commissions have done so.

Fights are put on in some states that don't even have boxing commissions. But under the new law, no professional boxing matches can be held in a state that does not have a commission, unless those matches are supervised by another state's commission.

"Allegations about possible abuses by promoters and matchmakers that have been raised recently in Oklahoma, Indiana and Missouri," McCain said, "are representative of the very worse impressions that the public has about boxing in America."

McCain said an investigation by Oklahoma authorities uncovered a "system of fixed fights, fraudulent bouts, phony names and manufactured records." McCain also cited allegations in Indiana that a boxer's 98-3 record involved 14 victories over the same opponent and a total of 12 over two other opponents.

For knowingly violating the new law, managers, promoters, matchmakers, licensees or employees of boxing commissions can be imprisoned up to one year, or fined up to $20,000.

For boxing's shady people, a prison term or those relatively modest fines will be worth the risk of doing what they have been doing all along. So without diligent enforcement, the new Federal law won't mean much.

But afer all these years, a Federal law exists that boxing people must obey or face the consequences. Finally!

CHAIRMAN
CRIME VICTIMS
CRIME & CORRECTION
CO-CHAIRMAN
NYS LEGISLATIVE TASK FORCE ON
DEMOGRAPHIC RESEARCH & REAPPORTIONMENT

COMMITTEES
FINANCE
RULES
CODES
ELECTIONS
INVESTIGATIONS &
GOVERNMENT OPERATIONS
JUDICIARY
RACING, GAMING & WAGERING
TRANSPORTATION

SENATOR
MICHAEL F. NOZZOLIO
54TH DISTRICT
SECRETARY TO THE MAJORITY CONFERENCE

June 2012

Mr. Ray Ciancaglini
5549 East Lake Road
Romulus, New York 14541

Dear Ray:

It was a pleasure to participate in the annual Geneva Sports Hall of Fame
dinner and to recognize your outstanding sports achievements as well as your
efforts to protect young athletes from head trauma injuries - the same kind of
injuries that you endured in your early years of boxing. You are to be
commended for wanting to make a difference in the lives of so many athletes.

Enclosed is a copy of the New York State Senate Resolution that I prepared on
your behalf. This formal Resolution was adopted by the New York State
Senate on May 8, 2012 and is a part of the official proceedings of the New
York State Senate.

It is my hope that we will have the opportunity to cross paths again very soon
and, in the meantime, please don't hesitate to let me know whenever I can be of
assistance to you or your family.

With warm regards,

Sincerely,

Michael F. Nozzolio,
Senator, 54th District

MN/jsg/ssk

CHAIRMAN
CODES

CO-CHAIRMAN
NYS LEGISLATIVE TASK FORCE ON
DEMOGRAPHIC RESEARCH & REAPPORTIONMENT

COMMITTEES
FINANCE
RULES
CRIME & CORRECTIONS
ELECTIONS
HOUSING
INVESTIGATIONS
JUDICIARY
RACING & WAGERING
TRANSPORTATION

SENATOR
MICHAEL F. NOZZOLIO
54TH DISTRICT
VICE CHAIRMAN, SENATE REPUBLICAN CONFERENCE

March 2013

Ray Ciancaglini
5549 E Lake Rd
Romulus, New York 14541

Dear Ray:

Congratulations on your endorsement by the New York State Athletic Trainers Association as the speaker for all of New York State during National Athletic Training Month.

It is truly a great tribute for you to receive this recognition and it is a result of your hard work and achievement in educating the public that you have been rewarded with this honor. It has been my pleasure to work with you in this mission and I look forward to continuing our work together to increase awareness of concussions and their affects.

In the meantime, if I can be of assistance to you or the Second Impact, please do not hesitate to contact me.

With best wishes.

Sincerely,

Michael F. Nozzolio,
Senator, 54th District

Best
personal
regards

Seneca Falls: 119 Fall Street, Seneca Falls, NY 13148 • (315) 568-9816 • FAX: (315) 568-2090
Albany: Room 503, Capitol, Albany, NY 12247 • (518) 455-2366 • FAX: (518) 426-6953
Toll Free: # 1-888-568-9816
www.nozzolio.nysenate.gov • nozzolio@nysenate.gov

Ray appropriately fist-bumping with Senator Michael F. Nozzolio at the Belhurst Castle Ballroom

2013 NYSATA-Sponsored Speaker for all of NYS – Book a date today!

- Ray Ciancaglini, a former boxer who suffers from chronic post-concussive symptoms and has become an advocate/public speaker to raise awareness about concussions and second impact/repeated blows. www.thesecondimpact.com

- NYSATA is promoting/sponsoring his speaking engagements in NYS to any interested group (e.g. ATEP/college, local AT org., school/district, clinic/hospital). He is often able to accommodate multiple speaking engagements in one day and is available on weekends.

- **To schedule an event with Ray for NATM (March), email NYSATA PR at** pr@gonysata2.org. Consider creating a school- or community-wide event or join with other local ATs/ATEPs to make it a networking experience!

State of New York

Executive Chamber

This is to certify that the pen hereunto affixed commemorates the approval of Senate Bill Number 3953-B, by Senators Hannon, Maziarz, Ball, Adams, Alesi, Avella, Carlucci, Fuschillo, Huntley, Larkin, LaValle, Nozzolio, Squadron, Zeldin; and in Assembly by Members of Assembly Nolan, Benedetto, Sweeney, Zebrowski, Rosenthal, entitled:

"AN ACT to amend the education law and the public health law, in relation to directing the commissioners of education and health to establish rules and regulations for the treatment and monitoring of students of school districts, boards of cooperative educational services and nonpublic schools who suffer mild traumatic brain injuries," which became a law on September nineteenth, two thousand eleven as Chapter 496 of the Laws of 2011.

GIVEN under my hand and the Privy Seal of the State at the Capitol in the City of Albany this twenty eighth day of September in the year two thousand eleven.

BY THE GOVERNOR

Secretary to the Governor

Proclamation

WHEREAS, Ray Ciancaglini retired from boxing in the early 1970's unaware of the journey he was about to begin, and

WHEREAS, years of sustaining countless blows to the head and multiple concussions pushed Ray to launch *The Second Impact* aimed at warning young athletes about the dangers of one or more concussions, and

WHEREAS, Ray took his pro-awareness message to the area schools by speaking to athletes, coaches, and parents about the importance of addressing injuries properly, being honest about their concerns, and following through to make sure the athletes are taken care of, and

WHEREAS, the signing into law of the Concussion Management Awareness Act is another step in Ray's journey to educate everyone about the dangers of not fully recovering from a head injury. This law prohibits any student who may have suffered a concussion from participating in athletic activities until they have gone twenty-four hours without showing symptoms and have been authorized to return by a licensed physician.

NOW, THEREFORE, I, Stu Einstein, Mayor of the City of Geneva, New York, do hereby proclaim, Thursday, December 8, 2011 as

Ray Ciancaglini Day

in the City of Geneva and would like to thank Ray for all of his hard work in helping to protect today's youth from serious harm.

Dated: December 7, 2011

Stu Einstein, Mayor
City of Geneva, New York

GENEVA SPORTS
HALL OF FAME

Site Navigation

Home

News

History

Nominations

Sponsors

Directors

Links

Contact Us

Search Members

Sport

Year

All

Biography — Ciancaglini Ray

Go to Listing

Ray Ciancaglini
Boxing
Geneva High School Class of 1969

Although Ray first made his mark in the boxing ring, his lasting legacy will be the contributions he made outside the ring. Ray was a very skilled and highly regarded boxer. He compiled a record of 31 wins (13 by KO) 9 losses and 4 draws as an amateur before leaving New York State to box professionally. Today however, Ray suffers from the effects of multiple concussions which he sustained during his boxing career. Although he was never knocked out or knocked down during his career, the irreversible damage was due to concussions that did not properly heal before he resumed training and the subsequent fights. He never took time to rest and heal. Today this is known as second-impact syndrome.

Today Ray is doing everything in his power to make sure young athletes do not end up like him. He formed The Second Impact, an organization aimed at teaching student-athletes, coaches, parents, and trainers about the consequences of not addressing concussions properly. Ray worked with NYS Senator Mike Nozzolio to get a law passed, "The Concussion Management Awareness Act", which prohibits any student who may have suffered a concussion from participating in athletic activities until they have gone twenty four hours without showing symptoms and have been authorized to return by a licensed physician. Other states are modeling the law to fit their own head injury legislation. Ray brings his important message around the state speaking for free for junior programs, high schools, colleges, and has been interviewed on both radio and television.Â Most notably are RBN National Radio, YNN, CBS, and ABC. ABC News recently featured a national story about Ray that was discussed on Good Morning America. The stories that ran in the Finger Lakes Times, "Looking for Gain from a Lifetime of Pain" and "Every Fight Was a War" won top honors in the Sports Department; the 2011 NY Associated Press Award and the 2011 NY News Publishers Association Award.

Ray has received many awards including the Golden Glove Heart Award in 1970, the Rochester Boxing Hall of Fame Jerry Flynn Courage Award in 2011, the Geneva City Council Recognition Award in 2011, and the Rochester Community Hero Award in 2012.Â In 2011 the New York State Legislature passed a resolution recognizing Ray for his efforts in the passage of the Concussion Management Awareness Act. He also received the State of NY Executive Chamber Award for his efforts. Ray's greatest reward however is in knowing that he is making a difference in the lives of young athletes.

SPORTS

SECTION B

LOOKING FOR GAIN FROM A LIFETIME OF PAIN

Boxing concussed Ray Ciancaglini's brain more than he knew, and he wants young athletes to avoid his fate

Nozzolio co-sponsors a bill aimed at concussions

By CHRIS MARQUART
FINGER LAKES TIMES

Ciancaglini

VARICK — Ray Ciancaglini can look at his trophy case and tell you incredible stories from his boxing career, even though he might not remember your name. He can hand you medals, awards and newspaper clippings, even though his hands shake from uncontrollable tremors.

Ciancaglini suffers from pugilistic dementia, leaving him alternately confused, forgetful and trembling with Parkinson's Syndrome-like shudders. It's the lasting mark of his star-crossed time in the ring, the result of layered head injuries that accumulated before the initial one had healed.

Now, 40 years after he left boxing behind, Ciancaglini is stepping into a new ring. He's trying to spread the word and fight back against the dis-

order that has so deeply affected his life.

Ciancaglini has founded a website, "The Second Impact," at www.thesecondimpact.com With the assistance of Dr. Jason Feinberg, the Varick resident is visiting local schools and talking with athletes. Not only is he addressing the severity of his own concussions, Ciancaglini is stressing the importance of treating the initial head injury and making sure it is fully healed before going back to the playing field.

"The game you sit out today could be the career you save tomorrow," Ciancaglini says. "All my life, in boxing, the old-timers at Singer's Gym told me to gut it up, to

■ See GAIN AND PAIN on Page 3B

By CHRIS MARQUART
FINGER LAKES TIMES

VARICK — From the beginning, Ray Ciancaglini's vision was to take "Second Impact" beyond the Finger Lakes region.

Already, his message is being heard in Albany.

Sen. Michael Nozzolio, R-54 of Fayette, is among a group of six state senators sponsoring a bill (S.3953) to help Ciancaglini's initiative reach athletes and coaching staffs throughout New York.

The legislation would require all athletes participating in activities sanctioned by the New York State Public High School Athletic Association to forgo any athletic activities for a minimum of 24 hours after a concussion is diagnosed.

"Ray is an outstanding

■ See BILL on Page 3B

Submitted photo

Ray Ciancaglini was dubbed "The Paladin Kid" during his time in the ring. This picture is on the home page of TheSecondImpact.com, a Ciancaglini-founded portal devoted to concussion awareness.

Varsity Club

Finger Lakes Times sports writer Joshua DeSain takes a closer look at the growing awareness of the concussion problem in high school sports on Page 2B. Geneva High School plans to have all its coaches certified in concussion recognition by the fall season, and Palmyra-Macedon has implemented protocols to help identify when blows to the head are severe enough to sideline an athlete.

GAIN AND PAIN

■ Continued from Page 1B

tough it out ... and look what it got me."

Ciancaglini has been trying to get his program off the ground for two years, finally launching his website last month. His wife, Patti, helps Ray maintain a Facebook page.

"I know Ray has been trying to start this and get through to people, and it is starting to work," said DeSales Athletic Director Ron Passalacqua. "People are listening. They are starting to become aware of the serious problems that can come with an injury of the brain.

"Ray is doing a wonderful thing to alert people and tell them how to look for the signs and prevent further damage."

Ciancaglini said the response has been huge.

"I was confident we could do this, but it's still amazing to me," he said with a hint of disbelief. "We have so much support, and so many people are stepping forward for the cause."

Ciancaglini will speak with the Hobart College football team during its preseason training in August. He'll interact with DeSales athletes during a school-wide assembly May 11. He is booked for the Romulus Central School fall sports meeting Aug. 14.

Feinberg said Ciancaglini's personal experiences make his message that much more important.

"Ray's situation is different," explained Feinberg, who treated Ciancaglini for six years along with Dr. Heidi Schwarz, a neurologist. "Boxers have their own dementia — it's people who basically got pummeled — but Ray has that awareness.

"There are more kids playing sports that get concussions than kids that are boxing. He wanted to help increase awareness and educate athletes so (they) don't end up with the syndrome."

According to Feinberg, the brain and nervous systems are developed during adolescence. A teenager's sense of invincibility and desire to play can lead to greater problems.

"You don't get a second-impact injury if you take care of the first one," Feinberg said. "Ray can show it sometimes: He can't think or his balance is off. He wanted me there to support him. People might ask medical questions, and he wants to have validation."

"Ray has his story, but he's got the medical staff with him to really back up what he's saying," Passalacqua said. "I've known Ray a long time, and anyone who falls and has a head injury should know about this. The concussion problem in sports — pro, high school or col-

lege — is a hot issue, and Ray is a living example of what can occur or happen if you don't take care of it and look out for the signs."

Romulus Athletic Director and Geneva football coach Mike Pane agrees.

"We think the angle Ray is coming from will be effective and will benefit the kids, parents and coaches," he said.

Mike Cragg met Ciancaglini years ago at Smaldone's newsstand. He knew some of Ciancaglini's story. As Hobart football head coach, Cragg knows the danger of head injuries.

"I thought it would be great for all players not only to meet Ray and know his story but also to hear the message behind his story," Cragg said. "Maybe for some of them, it will help with the decision on what or how much to say to a trainer or a coach."

Cragg has been helping with Hobart and William Smith Colleges' preconcussion testing. Keeping a "baseline score" helps trainers gauge or measure the recovery progress of a student-athlete. Often, a student-athlete might feel ready to compete, but the numbers tell a different story.

"Preseason tests and testing after they get (a concussion) ... we are doing the right things," Cragg said. "But to have someone who has lived through it and coming back too soon and the damage it can do and the effects it can have is a powerful statement."

"Look at me," Ciancaglini said. "This whole thing was preventable, but I didn't take it seriously then. My mother watched me destroy my noggin. She begged me to stop, but I was too hard-headed to listen. I don't want another parent to watch their child go through this."

The website discusses common symptoms and warning signs of a concussion. It offers excuses athletes might make in order to play. It offers common warning signs of concussions and has links to medical articles on the subject.

Ciancaglini said it's important to realize an athlete doesn't have to be knocked unconscious to suffer a concussion. He was never knocked down or out, so the thought of a concussion never crossed his mind.

He urged any athlete that might have suffered one to come forward.

"A student who is not honest about their injuries or conditions is a student at risk," Ciancaglini said. "I hope people use this website and the tools on it to do their job more effectively."

"We implemented baseline testing at Romulus last year," Pane said. "We think Ray coming here is a

good next step to come in and talk to the kids about the importance of being honest with the coaches and parents. There is no good in hiding anything."

That, Ciancaglini admitted, became his own undoing.

In the late 1960s, he was building a fine Golden Gloves résumé. Monsignor Franklin Kelliher, a Buffalo-area Roman Catholic priest, met Ciancaglini while he trained in Buffalo in 1968. Kelliher dubbed Ciancaglini "The Paladin Kid."

"I'd go anywhere and do almost anything to fight. I loved being in the ring," Ciancaglini remembered. "Monsignor would say I was just like the hired gunman in the 1980s TV show, 'Have Gun, Will Travel.' He said I was a gentleman, willing to travel long distances and taking on any fight even on short notice. The nickname stuck."

Ciancaglini suffered his first head injury in 1969. Between rounds, he vomited into his corner bucket. He finished the fight, winning by split decision.

He remembers the aftermath all too well.

"For days I slept and slept," Ciancaglini said. "I had this ringing in my ears, I had a constant headache and I couldn't hear a thing, but the old-timers at Singer's kept saying, 'Tough it out.' I didn't want to be looked at as weak, so I kept on going."

"Monsignor even told me once I had the heart of a lion, but the head of a jackass."

He guzzled Pepto Bismol to control his nausea and swallowed aspirin like candy to control headaches. Ciancaglini remembers when Olympic Trials finalist Rocky Cudney caught him with a shot to the head, another of his concussions. Another time, Ciancaglini had ingested so much aspirin his corner people couldn't stop a gash over his eye from bleeding uncontrollably.

"I think, overall, maybe three or four times I fought with a concussion and got another one on top of it before it healed," Ciancaglini said. "It only takes a few times before you can get yourself in really, really bad shape."

Ciancaglini quit boxing in 1972. The damage was irreparable, though only in recent years has he began to understand the toll all those bouts took.

"If we can get to the kids, and make them aware and help the coaching staff become aware, we can make a difference," Ciancaglini concluded.

Ciancaglini is available to meet individually with student-athletes. Contact him through his website.

Online
www.thesecondimpact.com

BILL

■ Continued from Page 1B

contributor to our community. He cares a lot about fostering athletic competition, but there is a growing phenomenon across the nation."

Nozzolio said, referring to concussions and the severity of second-impact injuries. "There needs to be additional rules by the state health and education departments to ensure New York is at the forefront of protecting student-athletes."

"This is such a huge step for what we're trying to do," Ciancaglini said. "To have someone at the state level who understands what we're going for to support us, I couldn't be happier."

In a letter to Ciancaglini last month, Nozzolio wrote that "concussion symptoms often take time to surface, and this legislation will allow for a more thorough evaluation of the young athlete's conditions."

If S.3953 becomes law, students would not be allowed to participate in athletics for at least 24 hours following a blow to the head, even if a trainer or physician has cleared an athlete. A blow to the head would be defined using current medical standards established within professional and college athletics, and by various centers for disease control.

"It's up to the State Health Department to gather that and form regulations," Nozzolio said. "Legislation will likely have little impact on club sports or recreational programs, but the hope is the pending state policy will be adopted by organizers of those programs.

"We're not trying to prevent play or stop anything. We are trying to make it safer."

Nozzolio said there is no clear indication when the bill's fate will be decided. He said the proposal likely will be tweaked by the state Senate's health and education committees.

Ciancaglini is confident of its outcome.

"If we truly are putting the best interest of the kids on the front burner, then there's no reason that I can see why this won't go through," Ciancaglini added. "It's for the kids. I don't want any of them to miss out on reaching their full potential tomorrow because they were too stubborn or proud today."

NRI Neurologic
Rehabilitation Institute
at Brookhaven Hospital

SPEAK TO A COUNSELOR
(866) 320-0194

Former Boxer Shows Young Athletes The Results of Untreated TBI

PAUL STONE | JUNE 26, 2013

Ciancaglini speaks to young football players. Photo courtesy of John Meore/The Journal News

We've made great strides in improving our understandings of traumatic brain injury and educating many about the effects of an untreated concussion. Almost every athlete in America has to sit through classes and seminars about brain injury, and most are tested before the season begins to help diagnose any brain injuries that occur as soon as they happen.

Maybe these advancements are the reason it is so disheartening to see studies like the one published in early May reporting that almost half of all high school football players – some of the athletes at the highest risk for brain injury – said they would try to hide their injury so that they can stay on the field.

A Boxer's Memory: Study Shows
6 Years in Ring Change Brain

*Ray Ciancaglini has memory loss
from his years as a boxer.*
By KATIE MOISSE
April 19, 2012

Though words and names escape him, Ray Ciancaglini said he will never forget the first time he saw Carmen Basilio throw a punch.

"My grandparents owned a restaurant and the bar room was filled with people watching the fight," said Ciancaglini, who was six years old when Basilio beat middleweight boxing champion Sugar Ray Robinson in 1957. "I said, 'I'm going to be Carmen Basilio.' So I went in the back, hung up a laundry bag filled with towels and napkins, and started punching."

Ten years later, Ciancaglini was on track to become a middleweight champ himself. But repeated blows to the head, and failure to give his brain time to recover, caused constant headaches, confusion and memory loss. Ciancaglini retired from the ring at the age of 23.

The long term consequences of combat sport are no secret, thanks to high-profile athletes like Muhammad Ali. But a new study suggests just six years of boxing can cause lasting changes in the brain, including shrinkage of areas involved in memory and cognition.

"We asked the question: Is there a certain degree of repetitive head trauma that the brain can tolerate, beyond which you run the risk of developing long term complications?" said study author Dr. Charles Bernick, associate director of the Cleveland Clinic's Lou Ruvo Center for Brain Health in Las Vegas. "And if that's the case, can we detect changes in the brain before people become symptomatic?

Bernick and colleagues followed 109 current boxers and mixed martial art fighters, using surveys to assess their fight frequencies and MRI scans to detect changes in their brains. The more fights, the more severe the brain changes in fighters with six or more years in the ring. And after 12 years, the number of fights was linked to poorer performance on memory tests.

"This raises the possibility of detecting brain changes before people are symptomatic," said Bernick, who is presenting the ongoing study at the American Academy of Neurology annual meeting this week in New Orleans. "If you wait for someone to start having symptoms and retire, you've bought the farm. You may not be able to do too much about it."

In Ciancaglini's heyday, boxers would worry about knockout blows and discount the flurry of smaller hits.

"The myth was you had to be knocked unconscious to get a head injury," said Ciancaglini. "We didn't know what concussions were back then; we didn't understand them like we do today."

Dr. Vernon Williams, medical director of the Kerlan-Jobe Center for Sports Neurology in Los Angeles, said concussion symptoms vary, and may not include blacking out.

"We define concussions from a clinical standpoint as an injury with neurological symptoms, such as headache, nausea, dizziness, forgetfulness," he said. "You don't need to lose consciousness."

Mounting research in boxing, football, hockey and military service suggests smaller blows can add up to have major consequences, including chronic traumatic encephalopathy, a progressive brain disease with features of Alzheimer's, Parkinson's and ALS.

"It's not just the big concussions, but the chronic accumulation of smaller blows to the head," said Dr. Daryl Rosenbaum, assistant professor of sports medicine at Wake Forest University in Winston-Salem, N.C. "We get asked all the time how many hits are too many. We don't know the answer to that question, but studies like this will help."

With his hopes of becoming a middleweight champion dashed, Ciancaglini went to college to become a gym teacher. But his "foggy" mind held him back.

"I failed pretty quickly, and my heart broke all over again," he said.

Memory lapses and hand tremors from his days in the ring made it impossible for him to hold down a job. Eventually, doctors diagnosed Ciancaglini with dementia pugilistica, a progressive brain disease caused by repeated head trauma.

"At first I got depressed and threw out all my memorabilia. But I came out battling 'cause that's what I do," he said.

Now Ciancaglini says he has a new calling: raising concussion awareness in young athletes.

"I tell them, 'The game you sit out today could be the career you save tomorrow,'" he said, reading a line from a recent speech to make sure he gets it right. "People come up after and thank me for telling them my story. It makes me cry."

ANALYSIS

'In the clearing stands a boxer...'

His boxing career shortened by the effects of concussions, Ray Ciancaglini has become a leading advocate of concussion awareness. He will speak at Canisteo-Greenwood tonight. THESECONDIMPACT.COM PHOTO

Though it happened long ago,
Ray Ciancaglini still "carries the reminders of every glove..."

By Chris Potter
The Evening Tribune

HORNELL — Ray Ciancaglini appeared to have everything going in his favor entering a fight at Syracuse's War Memorial in 1969.

An honors student in the classroom, he had built a reputation as one of the region's best up-and-coming middleweight boxers before even turning 20, and he was coming off a victory in Buffalo just the week before.

But something wasn't right.

He had caught a right hook to the back of his head in the third round of that match in Buffalo. Though it didn't knock him down, the blow left him temporarily dazed, his vision blurry. The volume level of the crowd seemed to fluctuate wildly, as if someone was cranking the dial of a stereo back and forth.

Former middleweight boxer Ray Ciancaglini, right, presents Hornell Superintendent Doug Wyant with a pair of signed boxing gloves in appreciation of Hornell's efforts to fight concussions. CHRIS POTTER/EVENING TRIBUNE PHOTO

Still, he toughed it out, eventually winning by unanimous decision. He woke up the next day with a headache and fatigue, but he attributed the discomfort to the hard-fought bout. He had committed to the fight in Syracuse, and he didn't want to back out for something as trivial as a headache.

The symptoms lingered right up to fight night.

Ciancaglini felt slow, and it didn't take long for his opponent to take advantage. Ciancaglini suffered another massive blow in the first round. He again battled through the rest of the match with a muddled mind. In a daze, he didn't realize the outcome of the fight until an interview with a reporter shortly after the final round.

Ciancaglini has dedicated his life to making sure that second big blow never comes for the youth of New York state.

His story was instrumental in raising concussion awareness, particularly the dangers of second-impact syndrome.

The state implemented the Concussion Management Awareness Act July 1, legislation that was largely inspired by Ciancaglini. He also founded an educational website, thesecondimpact.com, and gives speeches

SEE RAY, A2

to any organization that is interested.

Ciancaglini will speak at tonight's Canisteo-Greenwood fall parent/athlete meeting at 6 p.m. He also stopped in the Maple City Wednesday, telling his cautionary tale to Hornell faculty and students.

He emphasized that "the game you sit out today could be the career you save tomorrow." Getting back in the ring after unknowingly suffering a concussion the week before proved to be the beginning of the end of his promising career.

He began to miss school, failing classes and sleeping excessively. His mind was in a constant fog, and he couldn't explain why.

"I threw a whole career away for the sake of not missing one fight," Ciancaglini said. "What a foolish mistake. I challenged a concussion, and I got beat. It cost me my quality of life, and my future potential. With the education that we have today about concussions, permanent brain damage and its life-altering conditions are so avoidable. So avoidable."

Conventional wisdom at the time suggested concussions came along with getting knocked unconscious. Ciancaglini was never knocked down, let alone knocked out, so the thought of a concussion wasn't really considered. And the daily headaches? Just part of the sport, the old timers told him.

The symptoms didn't end when he quit boxing in 1972. Ciancaglini now lives with dementia pugilistica, suffering from constant headaches, confusion, memory loss and tremors associated with Parkinson's Syndrome.

Attitudes towards concussions have changed

since Ciancaglini's boxing days, and he's helped bring about some of that change in New York state.

"Through my story, my goal is to educate athletes about the life-altering mistakes that I made, with the hope that no one will suffer the same fate as me," Ciancaglini said. "Concussions are hard to prevent. You play clean and you play hard, but they're going to happen. (Second-impact syndrome is) when an athlete who has already sustained a concussion sustains a second concussion before symptoms from the first injury can properly heal."

The Hornell City School District has taken steps to protect Maple City youths from second-impact syndrome. Hornell is one of over 3,300 schools that will take part in a program sponsored by Dick's Sporting Goods.

Before kicking off 'the fall sports season, Hornell athletes will complete an ImPACT (Immediate Post-Concussion Assessment and Cognitive Testing) concussion test. This test provides a pre-concussion baseline of brain function. If players are suspected of suffering a concussion, taking another ImPACT test will tell if the player has returned to full health or not

The test can take around 40 minutes, said Hornell Athletic Director Scott Carroll — a wise investment if it can prevent a player from returning to the field at less than 100 percent. Suffering from one concussion leaves an athlete more vulnerable to a second, Ciancaglini said, and the effects are cumulative.

Hornell isn't just testing its athletes. The district plans to administer the ImPACT test to every student in grades 7-12.

"Dick's Sporting Goods donates the money to offset the initial cost of setting up the software, so that we can purchase enough licenses to test not just our student-athletes," said Hornell Superintendent Doug Wyant. "We've taken it a little bit further than

what Dick's is offering. We've gone out and purchased enough licenses to test every student in 7-12.

"We'll test our athletes right now before they start their seasons, but once school starts we'll be testing every child that enters the district in grades 7-12. You can hit your head at any time. Concussions not only affect your athletic performance, but more importantly it impacts your academic performance."

One of the Ciancaglini's mottos is "leave no doubt, wait it out." Concussion symptoms can surface hours or even days after an impact, he said, so it's important to err on the side of caution. A lingering headache, concentration problems and changing sleep patterns are just a few of the signs of a concussion.

"If we think something has happened, we're going to take the stance that it might have happened, and we're going to make sure it gets checked out," Wyant said. "One concussion is enough. If you don't fully recover and you sustain that second impact, you may be affecting your career and have that lifelong impact that Ray has to endure."

Ciancaglini presented Wyant with a signed pair of boxing gloves in gratitude for the school's efforts.

"Honesty is the most important thing," he told the Hornell students. "Your coaches, trainers and school staff are looking out for your well-being above all else, but you have to help them do the best they can for you. You have to be totally honest about your symptoms.

"Sitting here tonight, I was very impressed and happy, but not surprised, to see that this school system has implemented the impact preseason testing. That's a very good test."

The concussions may have hit Ciancaglini hard, but he has dealt a counterpunch of his own. Forty years after his last appearance in the ring, he has yet to be knocked down.

Unity Rehab And Neurology At Farmington

1160 Corporate Dr
Farmington, NY 14425-9589

Phone: (585)723-7972
Fax: (585)368-3119
www.unityhealth.org

FROM: Heidi Schwarz MD
2655 Ridgeway Ave Suite 420
Rochester, NY 14626-4296
Phone: (585)723-7972
Fax: (585)368-3119

DATE: 03/27/2013

TO: Arthur Equinozzi MD
200 North St Geneva, NY 14456
Phone: (315)787-5155
Fax: (315)787-5151

RE: Raymond Ciancaglini   **DOB:** 04/10/1951
Phone: (315)585-0001

Dear Arthur Equinozzi MD:

I evaluated your patient Raymond Ciancaglini for Chronic post traumatic encephalopathy.

Vital Signs
Weight / BSA / BMI

Time	lb	oz	kg	Context	%	BMI kg/m2	BSA m2	BMI %
2:27 PM	199.00			dressed with shoes				

Blood Pressure

Time	BP mm/Hg	Position	Side	Site	Method	Cuff Size
2:27 PM	116/84	sitting	left	arm	manual	adult large

Temp / Pulse / Respiration

Time	Temp F	Temp C	Temp Site	Pulse/min	Pattern	Resp/min
2:27 PM				60		

Measured By

Time	
2:27 PM	Mary Daigler RN

History of Present Illness
This 61 year old male presents with:
1. chronic posttraumatic encephalopathy (follow-up)
61-year-old gentleman with chronic posttraumatic encephalopathy related to repeated head trauma who requested a sooner appointment today to discuss some issues that are concerning him. On today's visit, he shared with me the fact that he was seen by a neurologist, Dr. Alexandra Feldman earlier in his career as a boxer. Dr. Feldman felt that his neuropsychological testing was

Ray's Diagnostic Condition as of March 27, 2013

not normal and forbade him from returning to the ring. He refused to listen to her. At that time, New York State was under a fair amount of pressure not to grant boxing licenses because there have been a few deaths in the ring. Therefore, the commissioner would not grant Ray a license. He then went to other states where he could fight. Initially he seemed to do well but his performance declined as did his reputation. He is feeling fairly guilty about the fact that he chose to pursue boxing despite advice to stop. The long term consequences of this have been not only been difficult for Ray but also for his family. Of note, Ray was never knocked out or even knocked to the floor during his boxing career. Therefore, his recurrent head trauma occurred without a diagnosable concussion, but clearly led to his severe chronic posttraumatic encephalopathy. At this point, he feels as if he lives in a chronic "brain fog" that waxes and wanes in severity from day to day. In the past, he has tried acetylcholinesterase inhibitors without any benefit. He agrees that his cognitive decline has been very slow.

2. parkinsonism

Ray continues to note slowness of movement and increased tremor particularly when he is stressed. He continues to deny any recent falls.

3. depression

Ray was very philosophical on today's visit. He claims that he feels like a "fujtive" and that he has been pulling the wool over pupils eyes trying to hide his deficits. His major concern on today's visit is the fear that he will become a burden to his family. He already feels as if he is a burden to them and he has compromised his wife's life. The purpose of today's visit was to discuss end-of-life issues with me. He continues to derive great benefit and happiness from his second impact efforts. However, if and when the time comes when he cannot perform these things or be fairly independent in his own activities, he does not want to linger. Apparently, he has a friend who has advised him that if this occurs he should either become homeless i.e. run away or have someone dropped him off in an emergency room without any identifying information. He realizes that being homeless is not a wise idea for him because he would not be able to get ropinirole which he needs in order to have any quality of life. I told him that his identity would be quickly determined no matter where someone dropped him off. I tried to refocus the discussion on his goals for end-of-life care and incorporating his wife into this process. Given the duration of time he has lived with this progressive cognitive and motor decline, I can certainly empathize with his desire not to be in a nursing home on a long-term basis. Although assisted suicide is not legal in New York State, it is possible in other states. By the time he needs to think about these issues, more options may be available in New York State. At this point, I have encouraged him to open up this discussion with his wife through the use of a health care proxy. He denies any suicidal ideations. He feels that his suicide is "a coward's way out". He is not interested in starting an antidepressant at this point in time.

All the Unresolved and Resolved Allergies:

Description	Reaction:	Comments:
NO KNOWN ALLERGIES		

Past Medical/Surgical History

Condition	Year	Procedure	Year
Dementia			
Headache, tension			
		5 knee surgeries left and right	
		Nose surgery	
parkinsonism			
		Lower back surgery	
Head injury			
		Upper back surgery	
		wrist surgery	

Family History

Yes / No	Disease Detail	Family Member	Name	Age
Yes	CAD	Family h/o		

Social History

The patient is right-handed.

Education / Employment / Occupation / Military Experience

Employment	Occupation	Emp Status	Retire Date	Restrictions
Kodak	factory worker	disabled		

Marital Status / Family / Social Support
Currently married. Has children: Son(s):1. Daughter(s):1.
The patient lives with opposite sex spouse.

Tobacco
0.00 pack(s) per day. Years of use: 0.00. Cumulative exposure: 0 pack years.

Alcohol
There is no history of alcohol use.

Caffeine
The patient does not use caffeine.

Review of Systems
Constitutional:
Positive for:
- Fatigue.

See History of Present Illness.
HEENT:
Positive for:
- Vision loss. The patient has blurred vision.

Respiratory:

Negative for cough, dyspnea and wheezing.

Cardiovascular:

Negative for chest pain, claudication and irregular heartbeat/palpitations.

Gastrointestinal:

Negative for abdominal pain, constipation, diarrhea and vomiting.

Genitourinary:
Positive for:
- Urinary hesitancy.

Negative for dysmenorrhea, menorrhagia, polyuria and vaginal discharge.

Metabolic/Endocrine:

Negative for cold intolerance, heat intolerance, polydipsia and polyphagia.

Neuro/Psychiatric:
Positive for:
- Anxiety.
- Depression.
- Gait disturbance.
- Headache.
- Insomnia.
- Memory impairment.
- Psychiatric symptoms.
- Tremors.

Neurological
See History of the Present Illness. See history of the Present Illness.
Psychiatric
See History of Present Illness.
Dermatologic:

Negative for pruritus and rash.

Musculoskeletal:
Positive for:
- Myalgia.

Hematology:

Negative for easy bleeding and easy bruising.

Immunology:

Negative for environmental allergies and food allergies.

The following is a summary of my physical findings:
Ray was quite philosophical today. He came today with note cards so that he would remember to discuss all the issues that were concerning him. He did not want his wife in the room on today's visit. Affect was discouraged and tearful at times. Voice was soft. No facial asymmetry or sensory loss with Grade 2 hypomimea. 5/5 strength throughout with normal bulk. Coarse rest tremor was noted in the R upper extremity. No pronator drift. He had grade 3+ rigidity in the RUE and grade 3 rigidity in the LUE. He was able to rise from the chair without the use of his arms. Gait was moderately slowed with reduced arm swing bilaterally. He was able to corner in 3-4 steps.

Final Medication List

Medication Name	Quantity	Refills	Pres Else	Description
simvastatin 20 mg Tab		0	Y	take 1 tablet (20MG) by oral route every day in the evening
Prostate Health Formula 15 mg-2 mg-160 mg Cap		0	Y	
multivitamin Tab		0	Y	take 1 tablet by oral route every day with food
aspirin 81 mg Tab		0	Y	take 1 tablet (81MG) by oral route every day
Vitamin C 500 mg Tab	0	0	Y	1 tab daily
vitamin E 400 unit Cap	0	0	Y	1 tab daily
hydrocodone-acetaminophen 5	90	2	N	1 tab three times per day as needed for

mg-500 mg Cap				restless leg symptoms. MDD 3 tabs
ropinirole 0.5 mg Tab	660	5	N	2 tabs q4hrs from 6am to 2 pm, 4 tabs at 5 pm, 2 tabs at 6pm and 2 tabs q4hrs thru night MDD 11mg
gabapentin 300 mg Cap	60	5	N	1 tab twice per day as needed for RLS

This was a fairly heart wrenching visit with Ray. He is clearly concerned about his future and potential decline with regard to cognition. He has watched this happen in many of his colleagues that were boxers. He is aware that the decline can become quite precipitous toward the end. I empathize completely with his desire not to linger or be a burden on his family. However, at this point, Ray's presence in his family's life is a blessing. I tried to reinforce that with Ray. I think he needs to have this discussion with his wife but it would probably be helpful if the 3 of us could discuss this together. In order to open up this communication, I have sent him home with a health care proxy to review and discuss. They will return to my office in 2-3 months at which time we will have further discussions about end-of-life care. At this point, I have reinforced to Ray that he is nowhere near needing to consider this option. He agrees with this. He promised me that he would contact me prior to any attempt to "run away" or pursue the advice of his close friend. Given the fact that Ray has never benefited from antidepressants in the past, I strongly doubt that initiating any treatment at this point in time would be helpful. Unfortunately, it's more likely to add to his "brain fog". I spent 40 out of the 50 min. with Ray discussing his current concerns, prognosis and end-of-life options. I plan to see him in followup in 2-3 months.

Assessment

Chronic post traumatic encephalopathy (310.2), Severe.
Parkinsons Disease, Primary (332.0), Stable.
Depression NOS (311), Fair control.

Thank you for the opportunity to collaborate in the care of this patient. Please feel free to contact me with any questions.

Sincerely,

Heidi Schwarz MD
Unity Rehab And Neurology At Ridgeway

cc:

Electronically signed by Heidi Schwarz MD on 03/27/2013 05:54 PM

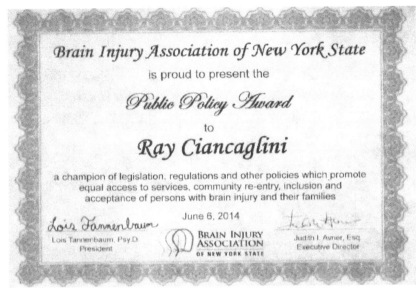

Brain Injury Association of New York State

is proud to present the

Public Policy Award

to

Ray Ciancaglini

a champion of legislation, regulations and other policies which promote
equal access to services, community re-entry, inclusion and
acceptance of persons with brain injury and their families

June 6, 2014

Lois Tannenbaum
Lois Tannenbaum, Psy.D.
President

**BRAIN INJURY
ASSOCIATION**
OF NEW YORK STATE

Judith I. Avner, Esq.
Executive Director

Ray was the Key Note Speaker at the Brain Injury Association
of New York State's Annual Conference in Albany, 2014

Ray joking around with actor Gary Busey in 2015 at the BIANYS
conference, who himself is a traumatic brain injury survivor

ROCSports

USA TODAY SPORTS NIGHTENGALE: MLB SERVES NOTICE WITH A-ROD DECISION **PAGE 10D**

Welker symbolic of concussion fight

I've long been a fan of Wes Welker, the Mighty Mite wide receiver for the Denver Broncos.

He was sand in the shorts of the Buffalo Bills when he played for the New England Patriots. Three of Welker's 31 career 100-yard games have come against Buffalo, including a 16-catch, 217-yard, 2-touchdown masterpiece in 2011. A performance like that has to be admired no matter the uniform.

Now Welker is set to return to action Sunday in an NFL playoff game against

Leo · Roth

SPORTS COLUMNIST
LROTH@DemocratandChronicle.com

the San Diego Chargers. A very durable player in the past, Welker suffered two concussions in a span of four weeks in November/December. Now, after five

See ROTH, Page 5D

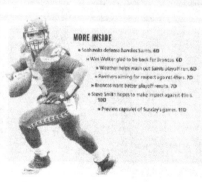

MORE INSIDE

- Seahawks defense handles Saints. **6D**
- Wes Welker glad to be back for Broncos **6D**
  - Weather helps wash out Saints playoff run. **6D**
  - Panthers aiming for respect against 49ers. **7D**
  - Broncos want better playoff results. **7D**
- Steve Smith hopes to make impact against 49ers. **10D**
  - Preview capsules of Sunday's games. **11D**

Roth

Continued from Page 1D

weeks total rest and getting doctors to sign off, it's time for Wonder Wes to play football again.

So why will I wince now whenever Welker goes over the middle for a Peyton Manning pass, working in those tight spaces as a slot receiver where the hits just keep coming? Why will I hope and pray that he gets up?

Is it because of the NFL's $765 million concussion litigation settlement with former players suffering from headaches, memory loss and depression? Is it because many ex-players ended their silent suffering through suicide? Is it because we know so much more about the effects of "second-impact" concussions and that a price has been put on glory? It's called chronic traumatic encephalopathy (CTE).

For Ray Ciancaglini, 62, of Varick, Seneca County, a renowned concussion awareness advocate and former boxer who suffers from dementia pugilistica, a variant of CTE, and Parkinson's Syndrome, a case like Welker's means one step forward and two back in this battle to save lives.

"I just pray for Mr. Welker because my God, a third concussion in such a short period of time could be career ending and could affect his quality of life down the road," he said. "This is coming from me. I'm not a doctor and I wish him well. But knowing what I know, there isn't anything worth the risk of a life of misery."

After following the NFL's concussion protocol, Welker was declared symptom free by the Broncos' medical staff and an independent doctor. Welker himself told reporters, "I think we've

Denver wide receiver Wes Welker suffered two concussions this season. CHRIS HUMPHREYS/ USA TODAY SPORTS

Former middleweight boxer Ray Ciancaglini raises concussion awareness through speaking to athletes like the football players at East High School. JAMIE GERMANO STAFF PHOTOGRAPHER

taken enough time. I feel fine. I'm ready to go."

But is he? A single brain trauma is said to double the risk for a future head injury (bingo). And two such injuries raise the risk of brain damage eight-fold.

Yes, NFL player safety is far better than when single-bar helmets were in use. But allowing concussed players to return to play so quickly makes me want to believe this whole protocol thing is just good public relations and legal butt covering. NFL brain experts say you can't manage concussions by a calendar. But when it comes to the mysteries of the brain,

common sense would say one week is pretty quick to return to contact even after a minor concussion.

Welker, after leaving a game against the Chiefs on Nov. 17 with a head/neck injury, was back in action Nov. 24 against the Patriots. Two weeks after that, he crumpled after a hit to the head by Titans safety Bernard Pollard. A second impact. A brain bruise on top of a brain bruise. Denver did shut Welker down, but only after two concussions, not one. And now he's back.

"The NFL's return-to-play policy appears to be very anemic to me," said Ciancaglini, who has taken part in leading CTE research at Boston University. "The policy should be that any player receiving two concussions in one season should be done for the year, period."

Ciancaglini, a promising middleweight whose ring career ended in 1974, has made it his life's mission to knock

The Post-Journal

www.post-journal.com

JAMESTOWN, N.Y.

FRIDAY

MAY 2, 2014

VOL. 97 NO. 348

B

The Post-Journal

FRIDAY, MAY 2, 2014

SPORTS

Inside

Scoreboard, B4

THE BATTLE WITHIN

'I Threw A Boxing Career Away'

Ciancaglini Tells JCC Audience The Dangers of Concussive Hits To The Brain

Ray Ciancaglini addresses the audience at Jamestown Community College on Thursday.

P-J photo by Jay Young

By JAY YOUNG
jyoung@post-journal.com

In his crusade to educate the public about the dangers of head trauma in athletics, retired boxer Ray Ciancaglini returned to Jamestown Community College for the third time on Thursday evening to present students and athletes with his lecture entitled "The Battle Within."

"The game that you sit out today, could be the career that you save tomorrow," is the motto that Ciancaglini tries to impress upon young athletes.

Since being forced to leave the world of competitive boxing at the age of 23 due to neurological damage sustained in the ring

"My life now consists of not what I want to do, but what I am capable of doing. I've had a headache every day since the age of 16, and I'm now 63."

— **Ray Ciancaglini**
Retired boxer

during a bout in Buffalo, Ciancaglini has spent his life visiting communities around New York State, free of charge, to tell his personal story of just how dangerous concussive hits to the brain can be.

While the former Golden Glove Team

Award winner and Rochester Boxing Hall of Fame member has visited the campus at JCC before, last night's speaking event included a screening of the acclaimed Steve James documentary "Head Games."

See CIANCAGLINI, Page B2

Ciancaglini

From Page B1

The film takes an in-depth look at the traumatic head injuries sustained by athletes across many different sports, and the research that is currently underway to better understand the effects and treatment of concussions.

"I threw an entire boxing career away for one fight," he told the crowd gathered at the Lenna Teleconference Theatre in Hultquist Library. "My life now consists of not what I want to do, but what I am capable of doing. I've had a headache every day since the age of 16, and I'm now 63."

A perpetually hard-nosed fighter, Ciancaglini was a victim of his own perseverance in the ring as he continued to battle opponents despite suffering from second impact syndrome — a disease caused by competing through multiple concussions.

"The belief back then was that you had to be knocked unconscious to have a brain injury," he said of his time in the boxing world.

While that belief may sound archaic and outdated considering what we know today about head trauma, the sad truth is that Ciancaglini continues to tour the state and speak to people because concussions are still underplayed.

"Never underestimate the powerful influence of peer pressure," he warns.

A main problem that Ciancaglini sees across all modern sports, professional and amateur, is the culture that has developed around "toughing it out."

Just as in the old days, athletes today are hesitant to admit that they are experiencing the symptoms of a concussion, and often hide their pain from coaches and teammates.

Worse yet, there are still plenty of athletes who wear their injuries, including concussions, as a badge of pride — what Ciancaglini calls "trash talk."

In his experience, there is nothing courageous about fighting your way through a concussion, especially considering everything we now know about the long-lasting effects of head trauma.

Repeated concussive hits to the brain have a huge list of terrible side effects, including dementia, chronic headaches, depression, anxiety, memory impairment and cognitive degeneration.

The only reasonable course of action to take when an athlete has even a slight possibility of a concussion, is to remove him or her from a game to seek medical attention. If head trauma has occurred, the only treatment for a brain injury is extensive physical and mental rest.

"My problems could have been avoided if I had known the consequences of a concussion," Ciancaglini reminded the audience.

Unfortunately, sports culture and industry have been slow to accept the dire consequences of chronic traumatic encephalopathy, which has become the most common medical term for injury from concussions.

That change is the focus of "Head Games," which chronicles former Harvard football player Christopher Nowinski's efforts to shed light on head trauma in athletics.

After leaving college, Nowinski suffered a severe concussion during a stint as a professional wrestler, and has since made it his goal in life to address the same issues that Ciancaglini speaks on.

Helping Ciancaglini and Nowinski to educate the public is acclaimed neurosurgeon, Dr. Robert Cantu, who is the clinical professor of neurosurgery at Boston University School of Medicine and a concussion expert.

Dr. Cantu is a leading researcher in the field of traumatic brain injury and heads the National Center for Catastrophic Sports Injury Research in Chapel Hill, N.C.

Ciancaglini has been participating in Dr. Cantu's research in Boston over the past several years, and will be donating his brain for study following his death.

Anyone who is interested in finding out more about resolving traumatic brain injury in sports may go to www.thesecondimpact.com.

Burke Hospital opens
brain health center for ex-athletes

BY JOHN GOLDEN
jgolden@westfairinc.com

At 63, Ray Ciancaglini still has the trim, muscular, compact build of a middleweight boxer. It has been 40 years since the upstate New Yorker was forced to hang up his boxing gloves and with them retire his dream of becoming a champion like Carmen Basilio, another upstate New Yorker whose epic Friday-night fights on television inspired a 6-year-old Ciancaglini to take up the sport. A member of the Rochester Boxing Hall of Fame, he fought both as an amateur and professionally in a 10-year career.

"My only regret as a boxer is that I didn't defeat my toughest opponent," Ciancaglini told clinical staff who stopped to hear his story recently at Burke Rehabilitation Hospital in White Plains, "and that opponent was a concussion. ... I challenged a concussion and I got beat."

"Lack of concussion education and peer pressure were my demise," the ex-boxer told his lunch-hour audience. "I've had 40 years to ponder it."

As he spoke, Ciancaglini frequently checked a script, his memory guide, set at an upright, nearly eye-level angle on a lectern in front of him so he would not lose his train of thought by looking down. It's an aid he has relied on in 20 years of speaking engagements on a personal mission to educate student athletes about concussions and help them avoid the "life-altering mistakes" he made.

"A program like this back in my day would have been so important," said

Dr. Barry D. Jordan and former boxer Ray Ciancaglini.
Photo by John Golden

the ex-boxer, whose large-fisted right hand shook with tremors as he spoke. Ciancaglini suffers from dementia pugilistica and Parkinson's syndrome. His brain, he said, will be donated after his death to the Boston University School of Medicine for the study of chronic traumatic encephalopathy, a progressive degenerative brain disease much in the news lately for its devastating impact on former National Football League players.

The program that brought him to Burke Rehabilitation Hospital was recently launched by Barry D. Jordan, a sports neurologist who is the private hospital's assistant medical director and former director of its inpatient brain injury program. Jordan has started the Retired Athletes Cognitive Evaluation Center, RACE, to evaluate and treat former athletes who are facing neurological disorders possibly caused by repeated head injury during their careers. He said the new center is collaborating with Mount Sinai Hospital, NewYork-Presbyterian University Hospital of Columbia and Cornell and Molecular Neuroimaging in New Haven, Conn.

Athletes exhibiting brain-related impairment later in life require a specially designed neurological evaluation. The specialized testing and treatment "can be very expensive," Jordan said, and some tests are not covered by Medicare or commercial insurance. RACE was started with seed money from Burke, but donations to the program are needed, Jordan said, to support Burke's commitment to evaluate and treat ex-athletes unable to pay for its costs.

Primarily a program for outpatients,

RACE also will allow former athletes to join in clinical research studies at the Burke Medical Research Institute on campus.

On his October visit to White Plains accompanied by his wife, Ciancaglini said he was having one of his good days. "On bad days, I struggle to tie my shoes or I forget the names of my friends," he said. Those days keep him homebound.

Because of memory lapses, he cannot care alone for his 2-year-old granddaughter. "This is the grim reality of more conditions to come," he said.

"I've had a headache every day since I was 16," he said. "I'm now 63. I'm constantly in a fog and I battle that every day."

At 44, the college dropout retired from his research department job at Eastman Kodak in Rochester, disabled by progressive dementia and Parkinson's.

Ciancaglini was a heralded teen prospect in what he called his "brutal and demanding sport" when he suffered his first concussion on his way to a unanimous decision in Buffalo. He quickly resumed training after the fight "even though I had a persistent headache and felt fatigued," he recalled.

Fighting in Syracuse, "In the first round I got my bell rung for the second time in a week," he said. "I was in such a daze, I didn't realize I had lost."

Ciancaglini said he was suffering from second-impact syndrome, a brain condition he knew nothing about in his boxing days. The common belief then was that a boxer had to be knocked unconscious to get a concussion. "In my opinion, the concussion that presents

mild symptoms, that can be the most dangerous," he said.

Once a good student, Ciancaglini began to struggle in high school with poor grades and behavioral problems. He slept excessively. But dosing himself with aspirin, vitamins and caffeine, he continued boxing, heeding an old timer's advice: "Gut it up. Headaches are a part of boxing."

"My relentless determination and desire defied all common sense and logic," he said.

Banned from boxing in New York in 1971 based on the results of an electroencephalogram, Ciancaglini entered the ring in other states "with less regulation or no regulation at all," he said. "I definitely circumvented a system designed to protect me." Fighting under assumed names in southern states, "I was a fugitive, you might say."

"I threw a whole career away for the sake of not missing one fight," he said. He said he would still pursue a boxing career but would seek immediate medical attention for any symptoms of brain injury.

"Downplaying the problem only increases the chance that an athlete will roll the dice when the wager far exceeds the reward," Ciancaglini said. That is the hard-learned lesson he shares with student athletes.

"The education part is just so important," Jordan said. In sports, less than 10 percent of concussions are associated with loss of consciousness, he noted. That can leave athletes like Ray Ciancaglini to think their head injuries are not serious and continue competing.

Sports

INSIDE
2B Scoreboard
3B MLB
4B Sports on TV
5B NFL
6-7B Comics
7B Days of Yore
6-8B Classifieds

METS TIE CLUB RECORD
— Page 3B

Friday, April 24, 2015   Finger Lakes Times   www.fltimes.com   **SECTION B**

Busy spring for Ciancaglini

Geneva resident continues to educate athletes about concussions

Times Sports Staff

GENEVA — Ray Ciancaglini has led a tireless quest to educate athletes, coaches and others about concussion awareness through his foundation, The Second Impact.

Ciancaglini, a former middleweight boxer who now battles dementia pugilistica, already has enjoyed a busy spring as he continues to tackle a long list of speaking engagements.

Ciancaglini

On Monday, the Geneva native will be the keynote speaker at the Washington State Traumatic Brain Injury Conference in Seattle. He will also be the featured presenter at the New Hampshire Traumatic Brain Injury Conference May 13 in

Concord, N.H.

Ciancaglini has made it his mission to make people aware of the damaging effects of concussions by telling his story. He talks about the way concussions were treated during his boxing career — it lasted from 1966 to '74 — and the impact they have on his life today.

He was the keynote speaker at the recent Burke Medical Research and Rehabilitation

Institute in White Plains. There he endorsed the new Retired Athletes Cognitive Evaluation Center. The RACE Center was founded by famed neurologist Dr. Barry Jordan, the director of the Burke Institute and Chief Medical Officer at the New York Boxing Commission Medical Advisory Board.

Ciancaglini will stay busy in the upcoming months.

He has been asked by

New York State Boxing Commission chairperson Melvina Lathan to address the commission later in the spring. He also will be talking to high school football players at four NFL Player Development Camps, stressing the importance of being honest about reporting concussion symptoms and being symptom free before returning to the playing field.

Ray is a member of Dr. Barry Jordan's RACE committee (Retired Athletes Cognitive Evaluation) and has also been a guest speaker at the Burke Rehabilitation Center in Westchester, New York. Dr. Jordan also holds the position of Chief Medical Officer for the *New York State Boxing Commission*.

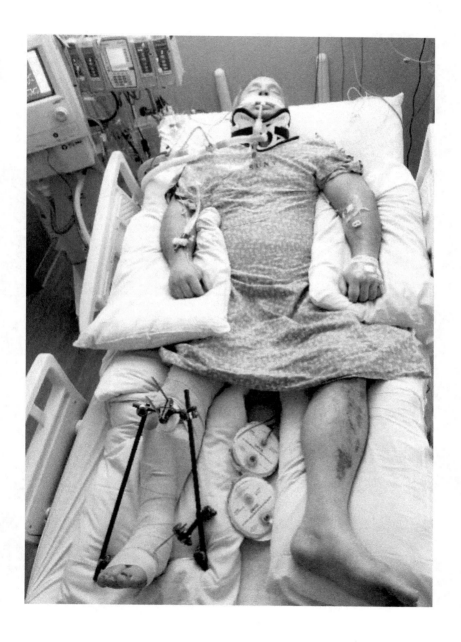

November 30, 2015, after Ray's car accident. Only a born fighter could win this battle.

BURKE
Rehabilitation & Research

March 28, 2016

Mr. Ray Ciancaglini
5549 E. Lake Road
Romulus, NY 14541

Dear Ray,

As a sports neurologist, it is becoming increasingly more difficult for me to ignore the plight of so many athletes whose long term medical conditions remain undiagnosed and untreated due to a lack of access or availability. As a result, we at the Burke Brain Health Center have created a groundbreaking program called R.A.C.E. (Retired Athletes Cognitive Evaluation) to address this issue. It is designed for retired athletes of limited means who have suffered brain injuries during their playing days. Its purpose is to evaluate their cognitive and neurological function and develop a rehabilitation program designed specifically for them. To date there are 7 athletes enrolled in the program.

We are in the process of forming an Advisory Council for RACE, comprised of former athletes, sports executives and writers and medical professionals who could lend their names, experience, insight and expertise to the program. Specifically, the advisory council would help promote the program and identify strategies to assist these athletes.

Enclosed is a draft proposal for RACE as well as other related material. I welcome the opportunity to discuss this with you in further detail and answer any questions you might have. Please email me to let me know if we can count on you to help these athletes.

Thank you for your time and consideration.

Sincerely,

Barry D. Jordan, M.D., M.P.H.
Assistant Medical Director
Burke Rehabilitation Hospital
bjordan@burke.org
914-597-2831

LET THE KIDS PLAY!

But concussion awareness, treatment need to be part of the game

By RAY CIANCAGLINI
Guest Appearance

In an Aug. 20 Letter to the Editor, Gerald Masters noted that Alan Brignall wrote a very inspiring article, "Teaching Safety and Life Lessons," that ran in the *Finger Lakes Times* on July 28.

Dave Marean, head football coach at Wayne Central, and John Evans of Mansfield University are both devoted coaches who for many years have taught safety on the field, especially concussion awareness and prevention and have been mentors to many youth, schooling athletes about life lessons.

I am very grateful that many changes have been and will continue to be made to make youth and high school football as safe as it can be. For example, I had the honor of speaking at the New York State Certified Football Officials Association annual conference about concussion awareness and am very pleased that they are proactively involved.

They have recently implemented a rule requiring that if they suspect a player has been concussed, that player will be immediately removed for proper evaluation.

John M. Crisp's syndicated column later, headlined "Definitely a Problem," is based primarily on athletes who have sustained many concussions, some not properly diagnosed or addressed, who in the long term, have developed Chronic Traumatic Encephalopathy (CTE).

I endorse and encourage athletes to play all sports. The attributes and work ethic principles developed through athletics will benefit athletes well beyond their playing days.

Concussion is an inherent risk of ALL sports competition, including not only football but others such as wrestling, lacrosse and soccer. Athletes accept that inherent risk. Concussions are hard to

■ See RAY on Page 2C

RAY

Continued from Page 1C

prevent. You play clean ... you play hard ... they still are going to happen.

But what IS preventable is when an athlete who has sustained a concussion sustains a second concussion before symptoms from the first injury have properly healed.

This is called Second Impact Syndrome, which carries with it a high risk of permanent brain damage and in exceptional cases can be fatal primarily among adolescents.

In my opinion, the concussion that exhibits mild symptoms can potentially be the most deceptive and dangerous. When the symptoms are mild, you are more apt to think it's not that serious, not report it and try to play through it, which puts you at risk for Second Impact Syndrome.

Early detection and being TOTALLY symptom free before returning to competition significantly reduces the risk of Second Impact Syndrome.

Numerous concussions increase the risk of developing neurological complications later in life. After your first concussion, you are more vulnerable to sustain a second and it is easier yet to get a third and so on.

The lifetime number must be monitored and extreme caution should be used when several concussions occur within a short period of time. The number of concussions an athlete can sustain before being advised to retire from contact sports remains a very controversial subject. Present studies remain inconclusive and further research is ongoing for a more definitive answer. Physicians handle each case on an individual basis with consideration given to the athlete's concussion history.

I am participating with several retired NFL players in the Legend CTE Study at Boston University because of my history of repeated, unaddressed concussions and I am grateful that my input, working with former State Sen. Mike Nozzolio, was instrumental in getting passed into New York State Law the Concussion Management Awareness Act (2010).

This law requires that all school personnel and coaches complete a state approved concussion course bi-annually and prohibits any athlete that has suffered a concussion from participating in athletic activities until they are symptom free for 24 hours and authorized to return by a licensed physician.

Concussion education is the key. Parents and coaches need to encourage players to be totally honest about their symptoms. My own son was a football running back from youth through Geneva High School varsity. Let the kids play! But if they get their "Bell Rung" have it addressed promptly and properly.

Ray Ciancaglini, a native of Geneva, is a former professional boxer and concussion awareness activist. His life story was featured nationally by ABC News and has been the subject of numerous award-winning stories. He has battled Parkinson's Syndrome and Dementia Pugilistica for many years as a direct result of numerous untreated concussions he suffered. He was instrumental in getting passed into New York State Law The Concussion Management Awareness Act, for which he was honored with the New York Executive Chamber Award and the Rochester Hickok Hero Award. He also founded the Second Impact Concussion Awareness Program (www.thesecondimpact. com) and tours high schools, colleges universities, NFL Player Development Camps and Youth Organizations lecturing athletes about the possible ramifications of not addressing concussions properly.

Ray with Dr. Bennet Omalu, who received high praise for his role in bringing to the screen the movie *Concussion*. Ray spoke with Dr. Omalu in Rochester in January of 2018 and presented him with a symbolic glove as a token of appreciation for all he has done for those suffering from CTE.

Megan DeRaps
Certified Athletic Trainer

March 20, 2018

Dear Ray Ciancaglini,

On behalf of Lincoln Academy, we sincerely thank you for coming to our school and speaking to our community. It's an honor to host you because of everything you do and continue to do for our students and students across the country. Your speech in the classrooms on bullying and character really hit home with many students. The attributes of being a good person such as; heart, courage, dreams, goals, determination, morality, and effort all resonated with them. These kids look up to an adult who tries to understand what they're experiencing and you my friend are that person. Many coaches and parents were very impressed with how well you spoke on behalf of your life consequences. You made the choice to turn your situation around by creating your foundation so that you can allow people to learn from your mistakes. That takes courage and heart to put your story out there for others to listen to. We noticed here at LA your passion to change lives. For that, we are forever grateful you made a difference in the lives of our students, athletes, parents, coaches, and our community!

Personally, I want to thank you for inspiring me to want to do better in the field of athletic training. After hearing you speak in November of 2017, I came back to Lincoln Academy with a new outlook. I wished the research was there and that someone had told you about all the negative consequences there are for fighting through a concussion. I knew that a lack of information and education at the time was the big factor. In today's age we have the ongoing research studies and information so you inspired me to educate! Creating this event, I believe, helped our community start spreading the word about concussions. It's not the end, but just the beginning of a shift in the times. I've had parents, coaches, and healthcare professionals ask me more questions, share personal accounts and ask when is the next one, we need to get more people to hear this message.

In conclusion, I can't write thank you enough times in this letter to show how appreciative we really are. You leave a lasting impression everywhere you go with all the lives you make better! Lincoln Academy will always welcome you anytime you're back in Maine!

Sincerely,

Megan DeRaps

Megan J. D

Ray and Patti—the happy loving couple

Rochester Boxing Hall of Fame
Geneva Sports Hall of Fame
Golden Glove Heart Award
Jerry Flynn Courage Award
NY Associated Press Story Award
NY Publishers Assoc. Story Award
NYS Executive Chamber Award
Rochester Hickok Hero Award
GHS Positive Impact Award
Camp Good Days Courage Award
Boston University CTE Legend Study
Geneva Rotary Club Paul Harris Award
NYS Concussion Management Awareness Act Contributor
Brain Injury Association of NYS Public Policy Award
Endorsed by the NYS Athletic Trainers' Association
Professional Boxing Safety Act Contributor

Ray Ciancaglini

THE SECOND IMPACT MISSION STATEMENT

Ray's mission is to tell his story of the mistakes he made not properly addressing a concussion and the lifelong consequences he suffered as a result. Ray's goal is to raise awareness, offer support, and encourage young people to be honest with care givers instead of playing through a head injury. Ray hopes, through his talks, that student athletes will understand the importance of addressing a concussion correctly and promptly. He encourages student athletes to be honest with symptoms and advocates following school or sport program protocols and doctor's orders to ensure a safe return to play.

Ray Ciancaglini has dedicated his life to educating and spreading the word to prevent even one more individual from sustaining an otherwise preventable brain injury from second impact.

Concussion awareness crucial for athletes

Ray Ciancaglini

Ray Ciancaglini's shares life experience, a cautionary story that can save lives

Ray Ciancaglini, a native of Geneva, New York, is a former professional boxer and award winning concussion awareness activist. [FILE PHOTOS]

Many athletes do not understand or take seriously the possible repercussions of hiding or playing through a concussion. They sometimes feel that they are invincible or that they are tough enough to gut it out. I was once one of those athletes. For many years, I have been battling Dementia Pugilistica and Parkinson's Syndrome. These progressive disorders are the direct result of my not addressing concussions properly as a young boxer.

The consequences of my actions have so deeply affected my life.

I endorse playing all sports but strongly stress the importance of being honest about symptoms and addressing a concussion properly.

I have been a concussion awareness and management advocate for many years and was instrumental in getting passed into

NYS Legislation the current Concussion Management Awareness Act. I also founded the Second Impact website www.TheSecondImpact.com which is dedicated to concussion awareness.

My speaking engagements, that include my real life story (featured nationally by ABC News), have successfully resonated with thousands of student athletes at high schools, colleges and sports organizations such as The NY Collegiate Baseball League and The NFL Player Development Camps.

My appearances are free of charge, last approximately 30 minutes, and I am not selling or endorsing any products.

References can be obtained from the many schools that I have spoken at such as Syracuse University, St. Bonaventure University, Mansfield University, University of New England, SUNY Brockport, SUNY Cortland, Ithaca College, Canisius College, Aquinas Institute of Rochester, East High (Rochester), North Rockland High School and others listed on The Second Impact website.

My awards and honors have included The Rochester Boxing Hall of Fame, Geneva Sports Hall of Fame, Golden Glove Heart Award, Jerry Flynn Courage Award, Rochester Hickok Hero Award, The NYS Executive Chamber Award, The Brain Injury Association of NYS Public Policy Award, GHS Positive Impact Award and The Camp Good Days Courage Award and the Geneva Rotary Paul Harris Award. My contributions were instrumental in getting passed into federal law the 1996 Professional Boxing Safety Act. My story was awarded The New York Associated Press Top Sports Story of 2011 and also awarded The New York Publishers Association Top Sports Story of 2011.

I have been endorsed by the New York State Athletic Trainers' Association (NYSATA). I have been participating with retired NFL players in ongoing Chronic Traumatic Encephalopathy (CTE) studies at the Boston University School of Medicine where upon my death my brain will be donated for CTE research.

I have dedicated my life to public awareness about concussions and am trying to reach as many young athletes as I can to give them the tools to make healthy decisions and I look forward to getting the opportunity to speak with student athletes, parents, coaches, school officials, and/or local community.

To schedule a (free!) speaking engagement or if I can be of any assistance, as a supplement to your school's concussion management program, please visit my website www.TheSecondImpact.com and feel free to contact me any time at 315-719-1031 (Cell) or e-mail at SecondImpactMail@yahoo.com.

Ray Ciancaglini, a former middleweight boxer, is a concussion awareness advocate.

A pickle barrel: a place where the lacto-fermentation of
cucumbers and the development of great men occur

ABOUT THE AUTHOR

Andy Siegel maintains a special commitment to representing survivors of traumatic brain injury in his practice of law. He is on the Board of Directors of the Brain Injury Association of New York State and the New York State Trial Lawyers Association. His many trial successes have regularly placed those outcomes among the "Top 100 Verdicts" reported in the state annually. A graduate of Tulane University and Brooklyn Law School, he now lives outside of the greater NYC area.

ABOUT THE TUG WYLER MYSTERY SERIES

Tug Wyler will thrust readers headfirst into the emotionally charged high-stakes arena of personal injury and medical malpractice law. At the center of each book lies the rush to cover up genuine wrongs. What keeps Tug digging deeper and deeper into the circumstances is his compulsion to make the system work for people at a disadvantage with their life situation stacked against them. Tug is unswerving in his dedication because justice is an outcome the big insurance companies—through their high-paid lawyers—vigorously resist.

Suzy's Case

When Henry Benson, a high-profile criminal lawyer known for his unsavory clients, recruits Tug to take over a multimillion-dollar lawsuit representing a tragically brain-injured child, his instructions are clear: get us out of it; there is no case. Yet the moment Tug meets the disabled but gallant little Suzy and her beautiful, resourceful mother June, all bets are off. When his passionate commitment to Suzy's case thrusts him into a surreal, often violent sideshow, the ensuing danger only sharpens his obsession with learning what really happened to Suzy in a Brooklyn hospital. Did she suffer from an unpreventable complication from her sickle cell crisis that caused her devastating brain injury? Or, did something else happen . . .

Cookie's Case

Cookie, an angel in stiletto heels, is by far the most popular performer at Jingles Dance Bonanza. To her devoted audience, she's a friend, therapist, and shoulder to cry on, all rolled into one. While meeting an old pal at the club, Tug doesn't expect to pick up a new client but quickly realizes the gallant Cookie—dancing in a neck brace, each leg kick potentially her last—is in need of a committed champion. Believing that Cookie is the victim of a spine surgeon with a sloppy touch, Tug takes her case. But as he seeks both medical cure and a fair shake for Cookie, he realizes—a tad too late—that sinister sights are now trained on him.

Nelly's Case

Nelly Rivera, when Tug first sees her, lies helpless in a hospital bed. Once sassy, active and ambitious, she's now a young woman with an uncertain future and a present seemingly tied to dependency. Discovering exactly what happened to her in a dental office while under anesthesia and who was responsible, however, is just one of Tug's goals. For he soon enough learns Nelly has recently inherited a hefty sum from her late father's life insurance. Which definitely complicates matters. The closer Tug, committed as always to gaining justice, gets to the truth, the more elusive it becomes.

Elton's Case

Wrongfully locked up for a crime he didn't commit, the wheelchair-bound Elton Cribbs's immediate situation soon goes from bad to tragic. Could it have happened that, while in custody and being transported with less than suitable care in a police van, he suffered the injuries that rendered him a paraplegic? Certainly, ever since then—for the past decade—he's led the life of an aggrieved victim, seeking justice while rejecting pity. Retained now to litigate Elton's case, even as the clock's ticking, Tug finds himself caught in the unlikeliest of conflicts. After all, what's he supposed to think when the defendant, otherwise known as the City of New York, begins offering him millions to settle while at the same time maintaining its allegation that Elton's case is a phony one?

Jenna's Case

A teen-aged girl can be among the most vulnerable of human beings. And the preyed-upon young woman at the dark center of Jenna's Case is certain to win the heart of readers. Believing Jenna Radcliff to be the victim of a Brooklyn doctor willing to put greed above his oath to do no harm, Tug takes on her case with deeply felt zeal. Yet what he quickly comes to understand is that his new client—once an obviously bright, outgoing girl (and ace neighborhood jump-roper)—is now a nearly mute shadow of her former self. As he proceeds to amass evidence against the conscienceless and defiant surgeon who'd willfully mutilated Jenna, Tug unfortunately soon discovers that the forces set against him are not only more numerous than he'd imagined but also more deadly.

Visit andysiegel.com for more about the books.

Visit mytrialguys.com for more about Andy's law firm.

CPSIA information can be obtained
at www.ICGtesting.com
Printed in the USA
LVHW080309020320
648560LV00001BA/1

Tema: Invierno   **Subtema:** Actividades de invierno

Notas para padres y maestros:

Los libros que lee su hijo en este nivel tendrán un argumento más sólido y aspectos que promueven el intercambio de ideas. En este nivel, haga que los niños practiquen la lectura con más fluidez. Túrnese para leer las páginas con sus niños y mostrarles cómo suena cuando se lee con fluidez.

RECUERDE: ¡LOS ELOGIOS SON GRANDES MOTIVADORES!
Ejemplos de elogios para lectores principiantes:
• Me encanta cómo leíste esa frase, sonó como si estuvieras hablando.
• ¡Qué bien! Leíste esa frase como una pregunta.
• ¡GUAU! ¡Leíste esa página con un tono perfecto!

¡Ayudas para el lector!

Estos son algunos recordatorios para antes de leer el texto:

• Usa tus ojos para seguir las palabras de la historia en vez de señalar cada una.

• Lee con fluidez y entonación. Lee como si estuvieras hablando. Vuelve a leer secciones del libro hasta que logres leer con fluidez.

• Busca ilustraciones y palabras interesantes en la historia.

Palabras que debes conocer antes de empezar

abrigos

bufandas

chocar

gorros

guantes

iglú

trineos

valla

NUESTRO DÍA NEVADO

De Robert Rosen

Ilustrado por
Brett Curzon

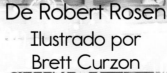

Rourke
Educational Media

rourkeeducationalmedia.com

Mira, hay nieve en todas partes.
¡Salgamos!

Hace frío afuera. No quiero enfriarme.

No te preocupes. Tenemos gorros, guantes, abrigos y bufandas.

De acuerdo, estoy lista. ¿Qué debemos hacer?

Bajemos por la colina en nuestros trineos.

Los trineos irán demasiado rápido.
No quiero chocar con esa valla.

¿Qué tal una pelea de bolas de nieve?

Tendremos bolas de nieve por todas partes. No quiero que la nieve me moje.

¿Y si hacemos un iglú?

Es demasiado trabajo. No quiero
sentirme cansada.

De acuerdo. ¿Qué quieres hacer?

Hagamos dibujos en la nieve. Luego se los podemos mostrar a nuestros amigos.

Dibujar no es divertido. No quiero aburrirme.

16

No hay nada que nos guste hacer
a los dos.

¡Ah, tengo una idea! ¿Cuál es?

Podemos hacer lo que quieras primero.
Y luego, harás lo que yo quiero.

¡Es una buena idea! Hagamos
un iglú primero.

¡Y luego dibujamos juntos!

Ayudas para el lector

Sé...

1. ¿Qué ropa usaron los dos niños para salir?

2. ¿Por qué la niña no quiere pelear con bolas de nieve?

3. ¿Qué acordaron hacer el niño y la niña al final?

Pienso...

1. ¿Te gusta salir los días nevados?

2. ¿Nieva donde vives?

3. ¿Con quién juegas afuera en un día nevado?

Ayudas para el lector

¿Qué pasó en este libro?

Mira cada imagen y di qué estaba pasando.

Sobre el autor

Robert Rosen vive en Corea del Sur con su esposa, su hijo y su perro. Da clases a estudiantes de kínder y primaria desde 2010. Le gusta viajar por el mundo y subirse a montañas rusas.

Sobre el ilustrador

Nacido en Sídney, Australia, Brett Curzon vive actualmente en la parte norte de Nueva Gales del Sur con su familia, su esposa, tres niños, dos perros y un gato malvado. El arte fantasioso de Brett Curzon se puede apreciar en algunos libros infantiles y hasta en botellas. Si no está trabajando intensamente, se le puede encontrar en el océano, o al menos a unos pies de distancia.

Library of Congress PCN Data

Nuestro día nevado / Robert Rosen

ISBN 978-1-64156-080-1 (soft cover - spanish)
ISBN 978-1-64156-150-1 (e-Book - spanish)
ISBN 978-1-68342-745-2 (hard cover - english)(alk.paper)
ISBN 978-1-68342-797-1 (soft cover - english)
ISBN 978-1-68342-849-7 (e-Book - english)
Library of Congress Control Number: 2017935461

Rourke Educational Media
Printed in China, Printplus Limited, Guangdong Province

Editado por: Debra Ankiel
Dirección de arte y plantilla por: Rhea Magaro-Wallace
Ilustraciones de tapa e interiores por: Brett Curzon
Traducción: Santiago Ochoa
Edición en español: Base Tres